Why I Write
Rosemary Catacalos

I write because the angry grandmother would nevertheless sing old Mexican songs about lost children in a voice that could break your heart. I write because an empty wire birdcage somehow creates open space in a crowded room. I write because it's the best way to pay attention. I write to remember laughing out loud when a white blossom tumbles from the Texas olive and a shocked butterfly chases it, tumbling too. I write when a good friend dies young and suddenly during an afternoon nap with his partner. I write because there is no corner of the world where human beings do not murder one another. No corner where history does not repeat itself. The ways we repeat ourselves at our peril. I write because in Palestine old women in heavy embroidered dresses rush to their fields to gather lemons from bulldozed trees. Also olives, oldest trees in the world. I write because every weed by every roadside is a miracle. I write because everyone has a story and every story could possibly save us. I write because half the world's 7,000 languages will disappear in the next one-hundred years and with them precious ways of calling "tree," "star," "mother." I write because language is our best and worst creation. I write because we have been given a sacred blue earth, and we endanger it and all its life. I write because the under-feathers on the breast of the Great Blue Heron are perfect down corkscrews, white spirals that keep the bird warm while she stands perfectly still in shallow water for hours. Such a feather hangs always above my desk. I write because my Greek grandfather arranged a marriage for me when I was twelve and was shattered when my father told him we didn't do things that way in this country. I write because my mother signed her high-school graduation photo "Beatriz," even though long ago her teachers had changed her name to "Beatrice." I write because it is the only way I know how to live, "… to mourn and castigate and celebrate all in the same breath."

ROSEMARY CATACALOS

On the Life and Work
of an American Master

Rosemary Catacalos: On the Life & Work of an American Master
Copyright (C) 2025 by Jim LaVilla-Havelin and Maha Ahmed.
All essays (C) authors unless otherwise noted.

ISBN: 978-1-7344356-5-8

Published by Unsung Masters Series in collaboration with *Gulf Coast*, *Copper Nickel*, and *Pleiades*.

Department of English
University of Houston
Houston, TX 77204

Produced at the University of Houston Department of English

Distributed by Small Press Distribution (SPD) and to subscribers of *Pleiades: Literature in Context* and *Gulf Coast: A Journal of Literature and Fine Arts*.

Series, cover, and interior design by Martin Rock.
Cover photograph by Jasmina Wellinghoff.

2 4 6 8 9 7 5 3 1
First Printing, 2025

The Unsung Masters Series brings the work of great, out-of-print, little-known writers to new readers. Each volume in the Series includes a large selection of the author's original writing, as well as essays on the writer, interviews with people who knew the writer, photographs, and ephemera. The curators of the Unsung Masters Series are always interested in suggestions for future volumes.

Underwriting support provided by Inprint Houston,
thanks to board member Debbie Gary.
Also by the University of Houston English Department

UNIVERSITY of **HOUSTON**

ROSEMARY CATACALOS

On the Life and Work of an American Master

Edited by JIM LAVILLA-HAVELIN
and MAHA AHMED

RECENT BOOKS IN THE UNSUNG MASTERS SERIES

2024
Tom Postell On the Life and Work of an American Master
Edited by Michael C. Peterson & Anthony Sutton

2023
Bert Meyers: On the Life and Work of an American Master
Edited by Dana Levin & Adele Elise Williams

2022
Jean Ross Justice: On the Life and Work of an American Master
Edited by Ryan Bollenbach & Kevin Prufer

2021
Shreela Ray: On the Life and Work of an American Master
Edited by Kazim Ali & Rohan Chhetri

2020
Wendy Battin: On the Life and Work of an American Master
Edited by Charles Hartman, Martha Collins, Pamela Alexander,
& Matthew Krajniak

2019
Laura Hershey: On the Life and Work of an American Master
Edited by Meg Day & Niki Herd

2018
Adelaide Crapsey: On the Life and Work of an American Master
Edited by Jenny Molberg & Christian Bancroft

2017
Belle Turnbull: On the Life and Work of an American Master
Edited by David Rothman & Jeffrey Villines

2016
Beatrice Hastings: On the Life and Work of Modern Master
Edited by Benjamin Johnson & Erika Jo Brown

2015
Catherine Breese Davis: On the Life and Work of an American Master
Edited by Martha Collins, Kevin Prufer, & Martin Rock

ADDITIONAL TITLES AVAILABLE AT
unsungmasters.org

THE UNSUNG MASTERS SERIES

UNIVERSITY of HOUSTON
inprint
INSPIRING READERS & WRITERS
gulf coast
A JOURNAL OF LITERATURE AND FINE ARTS
Cu 29 Ni 28
PLEIADES PRESS

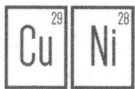

CONTENTS

Why I Write 3

INTRODUCTION 15
NAOMI SHIHAB NYE

Morning Geography 20
Crocheted Bag 21
Keeping the Vigil 22

For Rose on Magnolia Street 24
NAOMI SHIHAB NYE

This Broken Song 25
MICHAEL ANANIA

I WRITE IN THE MORNING 27
ANEL I. FLORES

Katakalos 33
A Dancer's Death 37
A Warning from Forever 38
Poison in the Eye of the Beholder 40
(There Has to Be) Something More than Everything 43
Final Touches 46
Ariadne III 49
Ariadne Seven Years Later 51
Daily Returns 53

*CONVERSATION WITH CARMEN TAFOLLA
AND IRE'NE LARA SILVA* 58
MAHA AHMED & JIM LAVILLA-HAVELIN, INTERVIEWERS

    the earth of us 66
    IRE'NE LARA SILVA

    Mr. Chairman Takes His Leave 68

*ON ROSEMARY CATACALOS'S BOOK
AGAIN FOR THE FIRST TIME* 71
REGINALD GIBBONS

*AFTERWORD TO THE THIRTIETH ANNIVERSARY
EDITION* 75
ARTHUR SZE

*POEMS NEW AND OLD FROM TEXAS POET
LAUREATE ROSEMARY CATACALOS* 78
ANIS SHIVANI

    Learning Endurance from Lupe
       at the J & A Ice House 82

ROSEMARY: POET OF THE WORLD 85
MAHA AHMED

    "and where are the women poets?"—a reply 92
    [Finally, the best things are simple] 94
    The Lesson in "A Waltz for Debby" 95
    Women Series I 97
    Sight Unseen 98
    Outcast 100
    Headscarf 102

Question to the Master on the Ways
of Synchronicity 103

ON COLLABORATING WITH ROSEMARY 104
CARY CLACK

Resistance: A Protocol 107
ROSEMARY CATACALOS AND CARY CLACK

POET'S VOICE WILL LIVE ON
IN WORLD SHE LOVED 111
CARY CLACK

THE ROSE CHRONICLES 114
BETSY SCHULTZ

ON MNEMOSYNO 121
BETT BUTLER AND JOËL DILLEY

Mnemosyno 122

A SEAMLESSLY COMMITTED LIFE 124
ROSEMARY CATACALOS

TRIBUTE TO ROSEMARY 131
GRACIELA SANCHEZ

Homesteaders 134
Women Talk of Flowers at Dusk 138
Memory in the Making: A Poetics 140
Perfect Attendance: Short Subjects Made from
the Staring Photos of Strangers 142

"PRAISE THEM" 144
POEM BY LI-YOUNG LEE
MUSIC BY ROSEMARY CATACALOS,
BRETT BUTLER, AND JOEL DILLEY

    Bop Physics I. & II. 145

ON BOP PHYSICS 147
MIKE GREENBERG

    David Talamántez on the Last Day of Second Grade 148

    Shelving Rose Catacalos 151
JIM LAVILLA-HAVELIN

    Red Dirt, Atascosa County, Texas 154

RED FOR ROSEMARY 156
JIM LAVILLA-HAVELIN

ROSEMARY CATACALOS: A CHRONOLOGY 160

CONTRIBUTORS 164

ACKNOWLEDGEMENTS 168

    In the Lands Where the Oldest Angels
        Have Always Known It Would Come to This,
        Aylan Tells of His Fleeting Two Years 184

THE UNSUNG MASTERS SERIES

INTRODUCTION

Naomi Shihab Nye

She was the most beautiful person we ever knew.

Beautiful in every possible way—physically, fashionably, domestically—a departing house-sitter once told her she had the most "overly-intentional" home space they'd ever seen, which bothered her for years. Each item was placed *just so*. Her voice rang deeply, elegantly low-pitched and richly resonant. Her manner of speaking itself felt exceptionally precise. When she traveled, she carried her beautiful goods in vintage straw baskets, never clunky luggage. Meticulous about her foods, her jazz and blues, her flamboyant loopy handwriting which took up a lot of space on a page, her one hundred rolled-up socks, her everything. I felt clumsy and under-dressed around her.

Rosemary sometimes verbalized the punctuation in her sentences. "Right on the street in front of my house, comma, there was an astonishing gun battle, exclamation point! And a bullet whizzed right into my neighbor's front room, two exclamation points!!" (This was actually spoken during our last in-person conversation.)

She started off as Rosemary, but as the years went by (comma), streamlined it to Rose.

Most importantly, she was beautiful intellectually. She knew more about everything—culture, history, poetry heroes, freedom fighters in all lands, geography, mythology, current politics, than anyone else most of us would ever meet—a realm of knowledge that felt vast and unstoppable. How did she learn all that? We met while I was in college—her sister Linda was in my Trinity University class, and urged me to call her, since Rosemary, too, was a poet. At our first meeting, I was 19, she was 26. She sat smoking, already married, in a small River Road neighborhood cottage behind a larger house, with a tree growing out of her bathtub. I stumbled around staring at things. Mexican folk art, tightly woven brightly colored Guatemalan and Mexican tapestries pinned to the walls. She seemed pensive, brooding. She did not seem thrilled to meet me, but somewhat suspicious, asking only a few questions, perhaps a little dubious about friendship. She would raise her eyebrows— "You don't say?"

I marveled that Rose had never gone to college at all, but moved from high school straight into working as a journalist. She was doing the police beat. This seemed avant-garde and brave. I always felt astonished that she seemed to know the first name of every waitperson in every worthy humble café in town and greeted everyone warmly. Any postal clerk! Each custodian in all the schools where we later worked! Every vegetable vendor and neighborhood vagabond and old-timer—each one was dignified with a name. Sometimes she spoke in Spanish to them. Her Mexican/Greek heritage felt deeper and more shimmering than any section of our famous little river, any wondrously mixed neighborhood, any story anyone could ever tell. And she kept telling it.

We worked as early Texas poets-in-the-schools, thanks to programs sponsored by the Texas Commission on the Arts, beginning in 1973-74 before hundreds of people in many other states did. I looked up to her as my true mentor (she had started a year before I did), and was always curious to know what she was doing in class with her kids.

She loved them, that was evident. She cared about them all more than it even seemed reasonable, since our relationships with them were transitory. She worried about their difficult lives and "small vocabularies." She encouraged them to use Spanish in their poems, or any other languages they liked. What was the future going to do with them all? We both had long dark braids and people in schools often mistook us for one another, which seemed more comic as years went by. Sometimes we pretended to be the other one. People acted more formally deferential and respectful when I was her. Beyond the olive skin and braids, we did not really look alike.

An early newspaper review once described her as being "frequently ill"—a comment she did not appreciate at all, though she did seem vulnerable to illness and was often hermitic because of it. An early bout with cancer foreshadowed the seven years of brutal lung cancer which would eventually take her life. In 1989, she became a Stegner Fellow and migrated away to California for ten years, later directing the San Francisco State Poetry Center. Our city felt quite bereft without her presence. I'd enter one of her favorite restaurants and think, I can't remember anyone's name at all. Thankfully she returned home and carried on administrative duties by directing the local nonprofit writing center Gemini Ink, among other community endeavors.

Her two marriages and other romantic relationships seemed, to a platonic friend, to be intensely passionate, turbulent, and short-lived—never lasting more than seven years. She felt dogged and haunted by betrayals. Before her death, she would instruct me to destroy all her papers and journals relating to any relationships. Whew! I had no idea, having forgotten many of her doomed alliances, but reluctantly agreed. I also said yes to sorting and dispersing her gorgeous, massive book collection according to her wishes (libraries, women's centers, schools, individuals, no Goodwill!) This turned into a dusty, painstaking process lasting more than three months and I could never have done it without the devoted collaboration of Betsy Schultz, her last partner and closest friend and caregiver for the final hard years.

To pitch into a shredder any journal belonging to one's 50 year plus best friend is not an easy act.

But I had to.

I was afraid I might find sad things about myself in those pages, but did not. (She could be tempestuous, did not "suffer fools," and definitely got mad at me more than once over the many decades.) I did, however, find she had saved the gift card from every gift ever given her, which made me cry and wish I had given her more. Each holiday she dropped off exactly the same gift—occasionally with an accompanying grapefruit or two from a local tree—some odd little golden bookmarks, attached to a card, none of which I ever used. These days, when they might feel tender to hold, they have all mysteriously disappeared.

But mostly, her poetry. Her unbelievably great poetry. Densely layered, exquisitely observant, eloquently thoughtful, profoundly humane poetry. No one ever wrote poems like Rose's—they seemed to spring forth so brilliantly textured, so well-paced and intricately woven—it was hard even to imagine writing poems with such deep twining roots. Filled with humanity, shining with voices and scenes and characters, they created a genre almost all their own in the vast realm of poetry—they belonged to deep time and difficulty and ways of continuing. They were valiant, glorious hymns to life.

And she refused to submit work to any publication which had not invited her.

About this we were diametrically opposed and there was no talking her out of it.

Invitations required.

Did she fear rejection? I think not. Maybe she just knew the quality of her work and did not want to waste time convincing anyone else of it, if they did not already know. I have never figured this out.

We are all so grateful to Jim LaVilla-Havelin, terrific poet, San Antonio community poetry teacher and activist, and Rose's literary executor extraordinaire, for compiling this beautiful volume with love and care, as we are all grateful for everyone else who contributed to it. The Unsung Masters Series, The University of Houston, and Inprint are doing such marvelous work bringing voices which deserve to be more widely heard to a larger span of readers.

Deepest thanks to co-editor Maha Ahmed for her great and loving care with this manuscript. Rose would have been utterly charmed and heartened to know you. And a special thank you to Kevin Prufer and Martin Rock, with loving appreciation for their work on Rosemary's volume and the Bert Meyers volume, which meant so much to me!

Later in life we come to accept there are many mysteries we could never unravel, both nearby and far away.

Rosemary's gifts were so many—so vast—so exceptionally her sensitive own—there would be no way to summarize them which might feel comprehensive enough. Her passion for justice in our world remained central. About Palestine and Israel she used to say, "How did anyone ever think this was going to work out?" Her openness to magic, delight, and quirky fun fueled her profoundly serious opinions about things—many things—everything. History and folklore grounded her daily devotions. The home she left held tender shrines in almost every corner.

San Antonio, 2024

Morning Geography
Rosemary Catacalos

for Naomi Shihab Nye

Suppose the flower rioting on my desk, its wild, shouting
yellow streaked with red and ruffled as an agitated jungle bird,

suppose this flower, large as my hand, could be pulled apart
and the sweetness wrung out the way we did honeysuckle so long

ago, rhyming summer nights with fireflies: This drop of honey
for courage, this drop of honey for love, this drop for anything

you are dreaming of.... Last night I dreamed a woman I love
(in Spanish we say dreamed with, *soñé con Noemí*) running flat out

through Texas sagebrush to save her Uncle Mohammed, who died
on a mountain in Palestine years ago, a hermit who wanted no saving.

Dreams are like this, make all things possible. The way just now,
still drugged with sleep, I supposed a loud flower could save us, tell us

something about sweetness when half a world away a man tends a fire
in the street before his tiny rug shop, a short distance from some broken

buildings. He breathes the thick signals of burning tires, decoy smoke
to make the bombers think they've already struck here. Suppose we could

have coffee with him, strong, laced with cardamom and small talk.
Suppose we'd figured out, on those immense and long ago

lost summer nights, how to get at the sweetness
without tearing the proud throat of even one blossom.

Crocheted Bag
Rosemary Catacalos

for Naomi Shihab Nye

Habibi, I want to love the string bag from Bahrain, a birthday
you say, with its brazen blue mouth and deep yellow light always
rising from below. Clearly a woman's work, stitches through which
the air shines, and the things within are apparent from without.
A woman's days laced together, closed only enough to contain
her faith. A woman's fishing net, her dream, which, if slept upon,
would mark the skin with equal-armed crosses that say the center
is everywhere. As grape leaves the world over are seasons with
the same sun. As no child anywhere should ever want to die. A
woman's prayer, with handles top *and* bottom so always the load
can be slung between two walkers on the same path.

Keeping the Vigil
Rosemary Catacalos

for Naomi Shihab Nye

The doors of the temple are ajar as
though a child had accidentally left
them that way. *People bring me
food, medicine, music.* Some dream
of me all night and also of giant
trees with visible roots. Others want me
to tuck white flowers into my hair
and dance on the poles of the earth.
Some even say they will pray for me.

"We *need* some dancing," you say,
alarmed at the hole slit sideways
in my belly, the hole that will
not heal, not stop bleeding.
Sleep now, little sister.
The pain will have its long feast.
but your fat candle, glowing among
all the other loved ones' charms
hanging from the roots of the tree, will
help me to see.

Soon the morning will open
again in the simple sighing
of roses, in the beating of goatskin
drums like hearts. Soon the table
will be set outside under the trees,

this time for the Easter feast.
You will hold my hand, reach
for another. We will dance,
all of us, in the sight of the stars
that can only be seen by day.
We will all be learning the moonstruck
skills of gauze and hot water
again for the first time.

For Rose on Magnolia Street
Naomi Shihab Nye

You ask me to remove my shoes
and it is correct somehow,
this stripping down in your presence.
Do you recognize in me
a bone, a window, a bell?

You are translating a child's poem
about the color gray.
I float through your rooms,
peeking at titles, fingering the laces
you drape from your walls.

The first place I visited you,
a tree grew out of your bedroom,
hole cut in the ceiling.
Today there are plants in your bathtub.
Their leaves are thick and damp.

I want to plant myself beside you
and soak up some of your light.
When the streetlamps cross their hands,
when the uncles shuffle home from the market
murmuring of weather and goats,
you lean into a delicate shawl,
the letters people write you
begin glowing in their baskets.
Yesterday you wrote of the dog-man
who wanders everywhere
followed by a pack of seven hounds.
Soon you will tell us the secret
behind our grandmother's soft hair.

This Broken Song
Michael Anania

for Rosemary Catacalos

98 degrees in San Antonio
   today, Rose, the sun breaking,
      now and then, through low clouds;

at the spillway, down river, swifts
   arcing, I imagine, above the foam,
      itself at once sudden and brief;

you are, as you leave us, all
   I remember you to be,
      certain in your affections,

love's insistences, like jazz,
   words that carry us along,
      a solo for tenor sax, certain

and implausible; we are left
   behind, loss all around us;
      who is there now to guide us

into song, to offer us, word
   after word, the place where
      myths collide, our grief

like masa, moving from hand
   to hand, the stone hot to the touch;
      they lean into their work, as we

lean today toward you, your voice
   inflected by Mexico, Coltrane, Miles,
      Greece even, the plaza, open now,

The Espada, all those devotions
   you presided over; can we talk it
      through, in your name, petal

after petal, straining with
   the day's heat, this morning's
      dew still held there, the slap

of tortillas, like castanets, dance,
   hands clapping; laughter, you said,
      is a kind of song, weeping, as well;

reach back to us, just once, the day's
   threads spun through your fingers,
      our singing, brightly colored there

I WRITE IN THE MORNING

Anel I. Flores

after "Why I Write" by Rosemary Catacalos

I heard Rosemary read "Why I Write" in 2013 and for several years asked her to please send me a copy. I waited a few years. It played over and over in my head. When she finally sent it, I printed it out and have carried it with me since.

I write because there's a Black Crested Titmouse perched on the fig tree right outside my window, boasting and big chested because they ate all the fruit again this year—and we weren't invited. I still love that Titmouse. I write because I have seen a Yellow and Black Kiskadee, an Orange Oriole, a Blue Heron, a White Crane, a Brown Pelican, a Green Jay and a Roseate Spoonbill all in one day. I write because birds talk to us. I write because I talk to birds. I write because there is space to describe the day I saw all those rainbow birds in one place. I believed it to be a magical, mystical message from our gay ancestors, telling me I can fly fly fly fly fly in every way.

I write because sentences are growing increasingly hard to craft together from fragments and acronyms of plenty. Because my students were supposed to be working on the journal entry titled, "I believe in [blank]" but instead were staring at their screens. I write because of Winterson, Rulfo, Giovanni, Kahlo, the kid who carved *I Am Gay* on the bathroom stall wall and because too much white out, too many fires and too many bans. I write because before I started writing they had hollowed out my core. I write because there still isn't enough, and we need more more more.

I write because love feels like the tip of my finger running across teeny tiny leaves of a Sin Verguenza tree. My father once told me on the other side of that leaf is the wind of your grandma Maria's ghost and her newborn sister, running miles to another rancho for help. Her mother was left behind. I write because the fascists overturned Roe v. Wade and the death toll for birthing bodies and babies is rising up up and up.

I write because my wife says there is a woman who rocks and reads by candlelight inside her window each night, but I have never witnessed it. You drive too fast, she says. I surmise, theorize, wonder if she is real, a ghost, or if her existence was meant for other eyes. I write because a migrant mother watches her child, while being looked down upon by a white coated doctor speaking words that bang like truck tires on a broken road that will never be smooth. I write because she still has to keep driving. I write because that mother is my wife and so is that woman reading a book. That little child, our children. I write because we just celebrated ten years of marriage, eighteen together. I write for our lives. For our lives. For our lives. I write.

I write because my braided thin rainbow bracelet doesn't dance and lament as loud as my heart loves to leap through the rear view and sing love songs to baby elephants, blueberries, baby queers, their cats, their dogs, their cuddle puddles, too. I write because it's one way to orgasm and despite the studies that say there are four to eight types, I'll find hundreds and thousands, all while loving the try.

I write because my mom describes her dress the day JFK and Jacqueline drove by on Broadway a different color every time. But the next day—like the black and white photographs—all remains the same. The nuns called out all the girls to circle the tv. We all felt like the world stopped. On our knees. We all cried, right honey? Was it 1963? I write because my father says watching her forget is like watching her die slowly. I write because they fell in love at seventeen and make it look so easy. I write because it wasn't easy between us for thirty years. Because the pen was sharper than the blade. It cut, carved and connected our hearts back again. I write because my 83-year-old mother and I both believe He Is Not Our President in 2025. He Is Not Our President in 2025. He Is Not Our President in 2025.

I write because it's funny that someone thinks they can rename the Gulf of Mexico, especially when we know she is Yemaya, Chalchiuhtlicue, Ganja, Tiamat, Galatea. I write because prophecy says the divine feminine holds the future of the world in her hands. I write because Sappho wrote poems to all of them, and I found some on the shore. I write because each time I weigh down my pockets with seashells and heavy regrets, the warm beach water takes on the color of all my ink. It seeps into the deep and I remember everything is vivid even after death. Yes, even after death. Yes, even after death everything is vivid.

I write because Rosemary writes, and plays and laughs and shares and loves and even sings to me posthumously through her poem. I write because every time I share it with writers, we write and write and write again. I write Rosemary into the Ebano tree that holds the Chalan Ferry at the Rio Bravo. I write that her words flower, fall, break through border walls. I write that her blooms make love to butterflies in mid-air through unlocked chain link fences with names like McFadden, Catacalos, Flores, Medina León, Shirof and Anzaldúa welded onto their open gates. I write because it is morning right now and right now and again and again it is morning. I write because the morning is my writing time and every morning we can start anew. Every morning we can start anew.

Katakalos
Rosemary Catacalos

The Old Man, we always called him.
We said it with respect.
Even when he embarrassed us
by wearing his plaid flannel work shirt
to church under the fine blue suit
one of his up-and-coming sons,
the three prides of his life,
had bought him.
Even when he spent hours
straightening used nails
when we could afford to buy new ones
so we could build the hundreds
of crooked little plant stands
that still wobble in the corners
of our houses.

He had come off a hard island birthplace,
a rock long ago deserted by the gods
but still sopping with the blood
of its passing from hand to hand,
Greek to Turk, Turk to Greek
and back again,
as if everything had not always
belonged to the sea, he said,
and to the relentless light
that hurt the eyes
of statues and children alike.
He was brought up on routine whippings
every Sunday, before-the-fact-punishment
to fit any crime. His father, the miller,
followed the wisdom that parents

can't be everywhere at once
and in seven days any boy is bound
to do something deserving a beating.
Besides, by his own admission
he was not a good shepherd,
always getting sidetracked caring
for some sick bird or dog or donkey
that followed him everywhere ever after
and got mixed up with the goats and sheep.

A draft dodger from the Turkish Army,
he braved the maze of Ellis Island
alone at sixteen,
escaping with his last name intact
and his first name changed to Sam.
New York fed him dog food
those first few months
when he couldn't read the labels
and only knew from the pictures
that the cans were meat and cheap.
He used to laugh about that.
Said it was just as good as some of
that Spam and stuff they sell nowadays.
Anyway, Sam was
the darling of immigrant flophouses,
giving away counsel and sometimes money,
always finding someone who was
a little worse off than he was.

He hoboed all the way to Seattle
where he pretended to be a high-flying carpenter
and was saved by *Hagia Sophia* from a fall that
would otherwise have meant certain death.
Then he came to where they were
burning Greeks out of Oklahoma

and anyone who could kept moving
and opened a hamburger stand
a little farther south.
In San Antonio he rigged up
a brightly painted horse-drawn
popcorn and ice cream wagon
and made the rounds on the West Side,
never quite making more than a living
since he always told poor kids
to pay him whenever they got the money.
The hamburger stands came next.
The cafe on Produce Row that some
old market hands still remember.
The Ideal Spot on South Presa,
where every hobo and derelict
from here to either coast
knew he could collect a free meal.
Good Old Sam.

But his wife was always angry.
She wanted a house of her own,
something more than glass beads.
She hated the way he was always
attracting winos and gypsies
and cousins from everywhere
who camped on her red velvet cushions
while he was out working hard
to give it all away.
She was from Lagos, Jalisco,
and when they'd met
it hadn't been so much about love
as it had been simply time to get married.
That's what she always said.
Sam never said much about it
one way or the other,

except to smile and tell us
she'd had a hard life.

Still, they must have had a
little something speical going.
Seeing how back then
he spoke only Greek,
a little broken English,
and she spoke only Spanish.
They were married through an interpreter.
Sam work an ill-fitting suit
and carried a brown paper bag
full of sandwiches he had made
so as not to let the few guests go hungry.

Years later when they were old
she had never learned English
and he had never bought her a house.
He'd spend years in his by-now-perfect
Spanish trying to get her to see
how there was always some poor devil
who needed just a little help.
When she complained the loudest
he just listened patiently
and went about setting out his
sugar water in bottle caps
to feed the ants.
A smiling survivor.
A fat soft heart.
The Old Man.
We still say it with respect.

A Dancer's Death
Rosemary Catacalos

in memory of Rosalio Ortega

Solitary.   Sombrero.   Someday.   Soul.
Leafing through the *Random House*.
Random leaving, going, gone.
Laughable how it all turns absurd,
how the worlds all run together
when a good friend dies.
Here on this page
and not in a hospital in Mexico City
is where it finally happens.
The meanings melt.   The moment
floats off by itself
no longer a part of my life
yet somehow still attached,
hanging by some useless Siamese
fold of emotional skin.
It's his death
starting at me from the far side
of a mirror in an empty dance studio.
It's caught me unawares.
I have nothing to offer it
but these ravings of an idiot child.
Why am I grinning?
Should I say something
about his long slender hands?
Is it too late for that?
Or too early?

Here on this page
a good friend dies.
Laughable lonely room.
Laughable old soft shoe of grief.

A Warning from Forever
Rosemary Catacalos

The latest manchild found dead in Atlanta
is floating in the Chattahoochee.
His name and age and favorite music
have bobbed away just out of everyone's reach
and he is tangled in the roots of a kindly tree
clad in a red garment from the waist down.
He had gone out that morning to sell
some old coins. This is all we know.
Not whether his momma always had to sweet-talk
him into eating his peas
or whether because he was small for his age
he was quick enough to beat all the bigger boys
at races. We don't know if he was apt to show off
from time to time just to get a grin from folks
or if his grandma could tell him stories
that would make talking drums go off
far far back in the blood.

Boy, boy, they might have said.
We've known a boy just like you
with his feet tapping the wet red clay
of the riverbank for the joy of it.
A boy with a barkberry and ochre
and the bright white of sunlight
smeared on his forehead in a magic pattern
that would make the finicky gourds fill
with water and the forest deer spirit
willingly give up its meat in our bellies.

*A boy who trusted the green shadows
of the trees as if they were his own people.
Boy, you must master this: the dogs know the air
around this village. They smell the thickness
of danger before it gets to us. Listen to
the intricate figures of their speech and
notice how they are careful with strangers.
Sharpen your own nose until it can slice
into every glint and ripple in the wind.
Know the precious signal of the hairs
standing up on the neck
and the low involuntary growl that comes
from deep inside the entrails.*

*Do this, boy. And do it well,
the drums might have said,
because the world is not always
as we would have it.*

Poison in the Eye of the Beholder
Rosemary Catacalos

I.
For some time now the hot brown city
has been impotent to touch me
except to call up disgust.
I am impatient with stooped old men
who take too long crossing streets.
I am unable to transform them.
They are embarrassing, graceless.
They are doing nothing but dying.
I grit my teeth at the regularity,
the sameness with which they
shuffle haltingly away to
pathetic rooms of faded gray
boards that lean and rot as they do.
They arrive to emptiness or perhaps
there are children and grandchildren
who shove them into corners.
Many must go home to wives whose
lips move incessantly, noiselessly;
whose eyes even in sleep are
rolling toward the grave,
whose knees bleed crosses on the floors,
who don't bother with shoes anymore because
they will never again leave their houses
or their constant prayers for death.
They send the old men out
to the corner stores for whatever
is needed to barely get by.
They send the old men out to drink
and act as scouts, as divining rods,

to attract the ghosts of dead mothers
and brothers and sisters.
The old men with their lives
coming loose from their bones.
The old men who don't remember,
whose days have matted together
like their dirty yellowed hair.
The old men always spitting
their untold stories into the dust.
The old, men and women, who are all the time
shuffling and praying and dying,
sores on the filthy skin of the world.

II.
Ancianos, forgive me.
All my life you have given me
songs and lessons and hope.
And now because I let myself turn
ugly, I fix you with a dead stare.
The love has gone out of my seeing.
Now because I have lost my way,
lost what you taught me to celebrate.
I betray you.
Ancianos, forgive me this failure.
You are innocent of it.
I do not deserve you.
It is I who have died badly.
I am the carcass,
the empty shell whose eyes and wings

and heart have been eaten away by ants.
Ancianos, if you will have me
I will follow the light in your faces
back to life,
and in time I might be worthy
of a death as proud
as the one you move toward
leaning on your sticks of courage,
singing into what is at the
other side of the morning.

(There Has to Be) Something More than Everything
Rosemary Catacalos

> *Oh, everywhere. All around. Trees are harlequins, words are harlequins. So are situations and sums. Put two things together—jokes, images—and you get a triple harlequin. Come on. Play! Invent the world! Invent reality!*
> —Vladimir Nabokov

But there are things that have been torn away.
From all of us. And we need to collect the shadows,
the pain as it ghosts along the soul in faded fragments.
We need to put as many old pieces as we can together
to make something else entirely.
As many times as we have to and as long as it takes.

There is for instance this mourning
I've been running from for six years.
My blithe floating off to Mexico
sure that time was in abundant supply
and leaving Albie showing the nurses
how to find the veins in his arms.
Showing them access to the bloodstream
the way only a junkie could know it.
Leaving him with a splendid view
of the Texas hill country and his own
short-lived certainty of harlequins and
most of his heart that would soon fall apart
trussed up into a series of blips
staggering across a hospital monitoring screen.
Leaving him knowing which words are the last
and how they should be spoken.

The story of death is infinite in its variety
but the end is always the same.
This time it comes with the impersonal
scratching of a long distance line,
someone saying, *Sit down and listen. Albie's gone.*

I clutch the edge of a hard bed in a hot hotel room
in an ancient country where there is nothing
at this moment except a senseless dead-end present.
No past. No future. Downstairs in the courtyard
a woman with a face older than the first sun forgets
and shapes corn into cakes intended only for the living.
The jaguar leaves his temple stone and his godhood behind
and lets his claws and teeth go soft with mortality.
The orchid suspends its sweetness
high in the canopy of the jungle
as if there will be no tomorrow
as if yesterday the young bride had not
fixed love into her hair.
To have come this far to see time snag and eddy
around my closest cousin's still-warm body.
To have come this far to watch him finally
drain away in that slow-motion torrent
he had always claimed as his own rhythm.

Today is six years to the day he was buried.
I know because Albert just called to tell me
that he's a little bit drunk and
that he's cooked up a batch of chicken creole
and why don't I come on over
and the damn calendar never just folds its hands
and waits like the rest of us
and yesterday was Father's Day
this year an even uglier black mark

precisely setting apart the hours
between the Sunday his firstborn died
and the funeral on Monday.
And we talked about growing old
and how the body begins to falter
and about the new camper
that sleeps two comfortably
and when not in use can fold down
to only six inches on top of the car.

And about taking Lupe and Sister Julia
to their hometown in The Valley
to visit an old aunt.
And about how electrical engineers have impatiently
taken over the functions of real watchmakers
without having an inkling of how to order
the true passage of time.
And about the sons who are left.
And suddenly there it is.
Something more than everything.
Everywhere. All around.
In the mundane inventions of our living
and laughing and grieving.
In the way we are somehow bound together
by this thing called family
that each of us celebrates so differently
but sometimes not so differently after all.
Just one stop on the way
to pick up a loaf of French bread
to go with the chicken.

Final Touches
Rosemary Catacalos

The third and last day given to us
is gray. We are not surprised.
We rise separately, dress in different rooms,
avoid looking at one another
except in the safe distance of the mirror
and then only briefly.
The glint of your silver shaving brush
is quicker this morning, having
so little light to catch.
It is as if God had grown
a tin eye overnight.
It is as if the whole world could go blind
in sympathy watching us trying to put everything
away without touching it,
watching us fail so miserably.
You tell me how you will pack your books
and I think it is the same story I've heard
since childhood,
the one with the moral
about how to laugh at the end.
I leave you at the corner
searching for something to carry you away.
No tears on either side.
By the time I let myself look back
you're gone and it's too late
to be turned to stone or to salt.

I remain conventionally human,
having to drag this bulging grief around
in its same used skin,

its same divided cells.
I try to remember joy.
I try to remember seven years ago in Spain,
the sea pressing in on all sides,
the olive trees and almond-heavy air
always forcing us together,
always forcing us apart at the last minute.
I try to remember the first
and only kiss before now,
a promise in the dark stairwell
of a Paris hotel named after
a martyr who died by fire.

I try to remember all the fond waiting
since then, the certainty we shared.
The drunken phone calls at holidays
and times of crisis.
The poems and birds crossing and
re-crossing the continent between us,
now north toward stamina, now south toward grace.
I try to remember finally rushing
into the arms of these last three days,
how at first we stood dumbfounded,
how quickly we learned abandon
and rose out of ourselves
and became one overwhelming thing
and shouted and shouted
like open country.
I try to remember how perfectly
we both rode out over the edge

of the world at long last,
past the open mouths of astonished stars
and every possible invention of beauty.

I try to remember these things
and in some ways I succeed after all.
This is what I know how to do.
This poem, this rude crutch I use
to limp toward whatever else there is.
I'm not new in this business.
I know how to carve my own heart,
lean from fat, fruit from sorrow,
flower from seed and vice versa.
I who sing so much about being woman.
I who believe in worshipping my ancestors,
in the serious game of enchantment,
in the ultimate triumph of memory.
When I feel myself beginning to stoop
too heavily, I catch my head
and throw it back on the sky.
Then the fact remains that I love you.
I love you
and sea stones in hot countries
and old produce vendors who carry
small ready change in their ears
and so much more.
Gracias a la vida.
The old-time moral about how to laugh
begins to take hold again.

Ariadne III
Rosemary Catacalos

Perhaps the string I send out
is a little faded,
going as it does through the mails.
There is no failure in this.
Time passes in the usual manner.
Some things happen. Others don't.

All right, it's true. My power
has grown somewhat weaker.
I have to face it when you say
your poems these days are addressed
to no one, or to anyone,
as if you would refuse if I should send
you out in the rain to look for angels.

Perhaps that's why I spend my days
in closets with my eyes shut, fingering
pairs and pairs of my worn out shoes.
Not that I've gone blind.
It's just that I've misplaced a secret
that's more like skin than anything else,
one that must be felt rather than seen.
Leather, the shape of a heel, a button,
a strap. The ways of the maze,
the loose footfall of our past, are
in these shoes. I have only to touch
them enough to reclaim everything.

Still, it's hard work, all this touching.
Nights I get drunk and have to ask

the names of common objects. I careen
into walls while trying to dance
and become terrified at the silence
of birds going deaf at my door.
I call up the bull and a lamb appears,
too feeble to carry the heavy horns,
much less draw the blood of love.
But you won't see me giving up.
This is still my parents' house,
a space given us by the gods
for the rekindling of spells.

Be advised.
Even if your letters are much too polite.
Even if you confuse your neighbor's
breasts with mine. I am still Ariadne.
I will hand you the pipes and make you play,
and I will make you dance again as well.

Ariadne Seven Years Later
Rosemary Catacalos

for G.

I suppose I don't have to tell you. You
already know it's my turn. And you must also
know it's been exactly seven years to the day
since you began learning, slowly you said,
the hatred I required of you, my eyes
that would not open, the mazes that would not end,
your fear that I was collecting you, that I rattled
the walls of the labyrinth only when it suited me.
Do you remember saying these things? June 16, 1976.

Yes, it's my turn. The minotaur is gone, the *real*
monster has fled. (You were never that, Theseus, no
matter what I've ever seemed to be telling you.)
The minotaur is gone. My love
has finally and violently tired of too many questions,
too much waiting for me to make
of him the lamb, the man, the *whole*,
the one thing or the other.

And so, he has crashed through the walls in a blind rage.
And the bellowing and howling is terrible. Since even
now, at his moment of breaking free, he cannot
speak, cannot say how I have failed him. Even now
when he gores me deep, decorating his wedding crown
with my blood. Even now when he tries to root out
my heart, that imperfect chalice, and offer it back
to my father in some kind of unholy tribute.
I'm telling you, he can't *speak*.

It has come to this: I have never left my father's
island. A shade followed you to Naxos, gave herself
to Dionysios, wears the garland of stars. I spend most
days lying on the floor of the maze, trying to stanch
the flow of my blood down all its blind alleys. My
only gauze is my one pitiful thread, recalled now
into a hopelessly tangled mess. Sometimes, in the early
mornings, I limp into the palace gardens and cut red
and yellow carnations, some fragrant basil, try to keep
them safe in the still turquoise vase of the sea.

                      Twilights are the worst.
That is when I stand at my father's highest window
watching the water for the tiniest sign of a swimmer,
keeping the tense vigil for the shaggy head coming back
to me. It is at twilight that I have shattered
my entire collection of spyglasses. Their salty
splinters are lodged in my hands, the hands
you always found so beautiful as they reeled out, reeled
in my little string.

                    No, Theseus, I tell you I am dying.
And yet I cannot. As you know perhaps better than
anyone. There are these words that must be spoken.
There are heroes to be remembered, heroines to be recreated.
The bloodletting has to stop. I need to lie on my back
in the sand, the white sun in my mouth, on my breasts.
I need to flap my arms the way children do in the snow
of colder climes. Make a sand angel. Watch her fly.

Daily Returns
Rosemary Catacalos

> *Well, it don't mean a thing if it ain't got that swing.*
> —Duke Ellington

So it's not that we *relearn* faith every
day. It's that we need to reassign it. In
that sense, Penelope was right. Every day
doing and undoing the whole cloth. The middle,
of course, would always be more tightly woven
than the edges. And there would always be stray
threads. One takes this sort of thing for granted.

Knowing there is always the possibility
of that moment of paralysis when one freezes *because*
of what one knows *and* in spite of it, like the mouse
staring into the eyes of a snake or the black dog
whose eyes glow red in the headlights of an onrushing
car. That moment of paralysis just before one either
flies or dies. It's that simple.

It's why my handprint on the glass coffee table top
is meant to keep the evil spirits away. It's why
my sister thinks she has to learn how to charm snakes,
tell fortunes. She fixes airplanes in her spare time.
Flies with and without a motor, solo or with friends.
It's all the same to her.

Here in this house we so easily call *The Resort*,
we are reassigning something. It's about a dog
who, early on after he was born, was named *Cerberus*
and then a few days later was renamed *Crowley*. This
dog is now eleven years old, has gone from black
to white, is blind, toothless. Chances are he doesn't

even remember his original name. But he doesn't give
up. He keeps trying to remember, I tell you. Amazing!

It's about how to let love, like names and lightning, go.
How to let it strike where it will. Penelope is in this
somewhere. Also Brazilian musicians who are just trying
to have a good time. And that Old Master of Matter Hans
Boltzmann, who killed himself because he just couldn't
get people to see how energy is an infinity symbol. How
our lives are like that, always doubling back on themselves,
chasing their own tails. Geoffrey said it this way
once: "The events of our lives are not our lives,
the way they throw us around."

It's all we have ever been trying to convince ourselves
is true. It's why we write these poems, fill the air up
with music. It's the only reason we are ever able to look
one another in the eye and be afraid and still say *yes*!

It's why we do our part, change shifts when we have to,
learn how to sort the garbage harmoniously, glass in one
bag, paper in the other. Like when we were children
and played at *scissors cut paper, but paper covers stone*.
What appears to be a simple game of chance. When that
is the thing it most is not. Any candle can be lit
at both ends. The trick is not to disfigure oneself
in the process. Like Albéniz, that scavenger among
the plenty of the olive trees, who dragged his huge
sorrow around for whatever it was worth. And lived to
sing about it. It's like you when you say, "Well,
you know, light and sound are the same thing, only at
different speeds. . . . You didn't eat breakfast."
Thank you, maestro. Now we're really starting to swing.

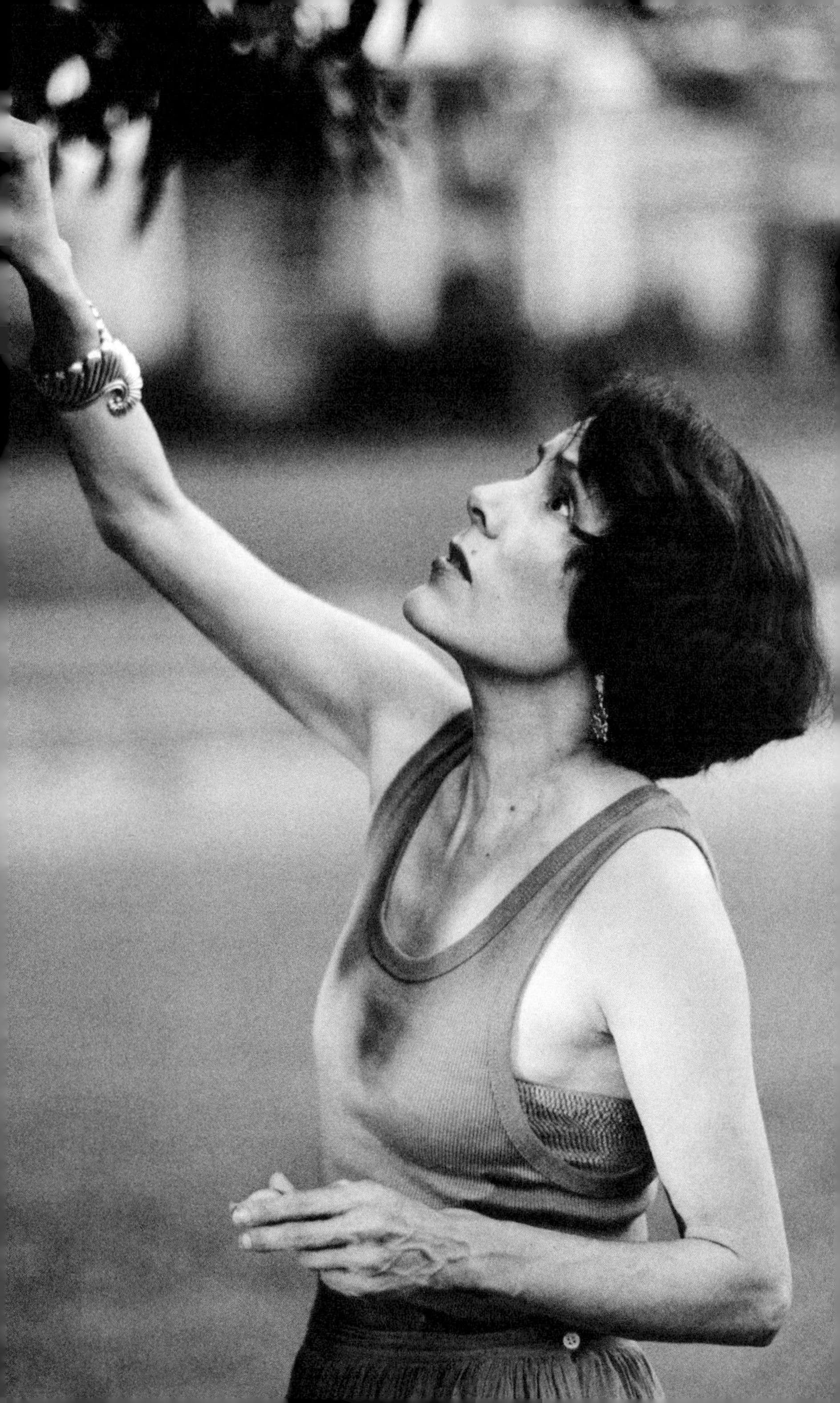

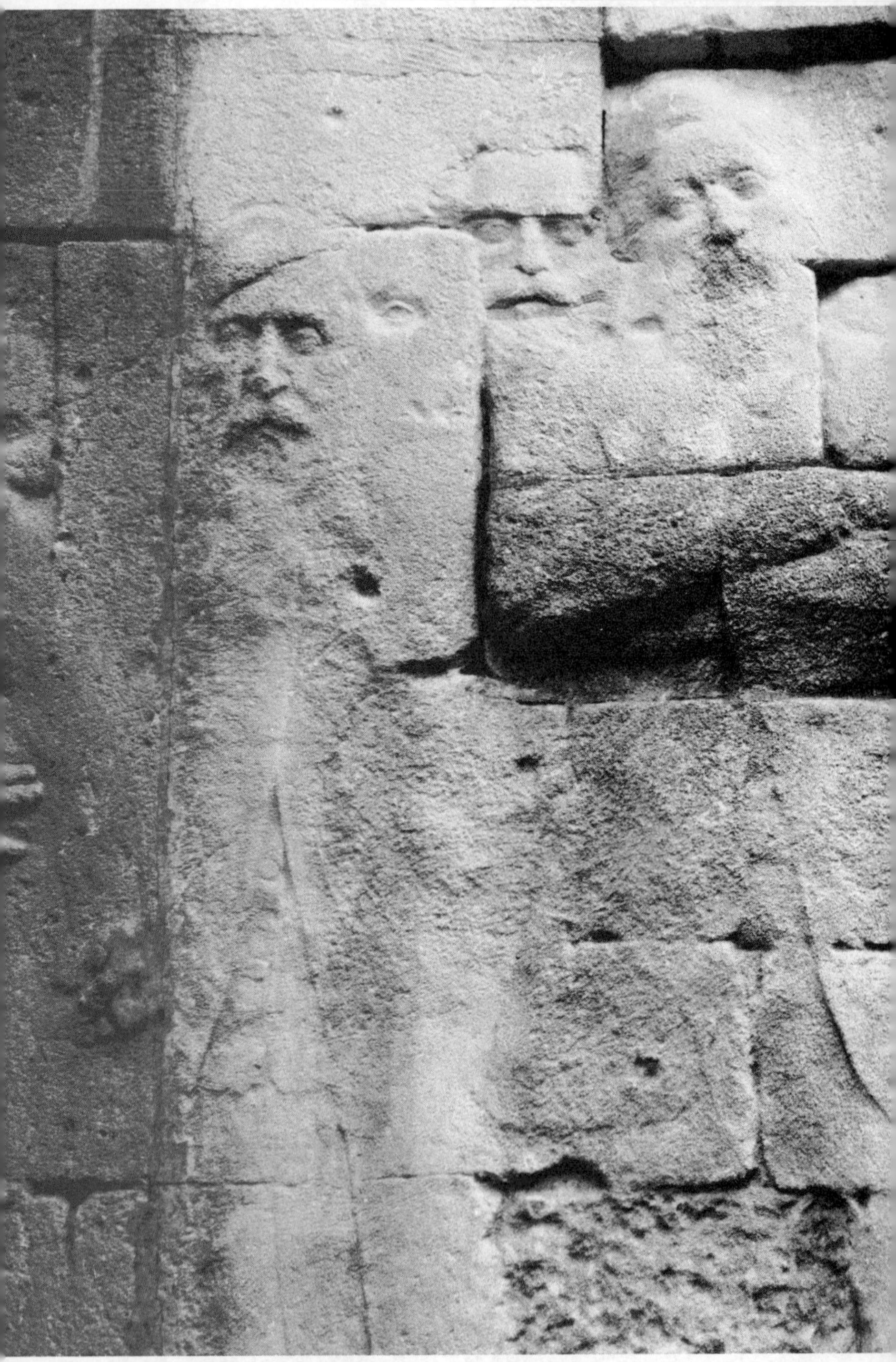

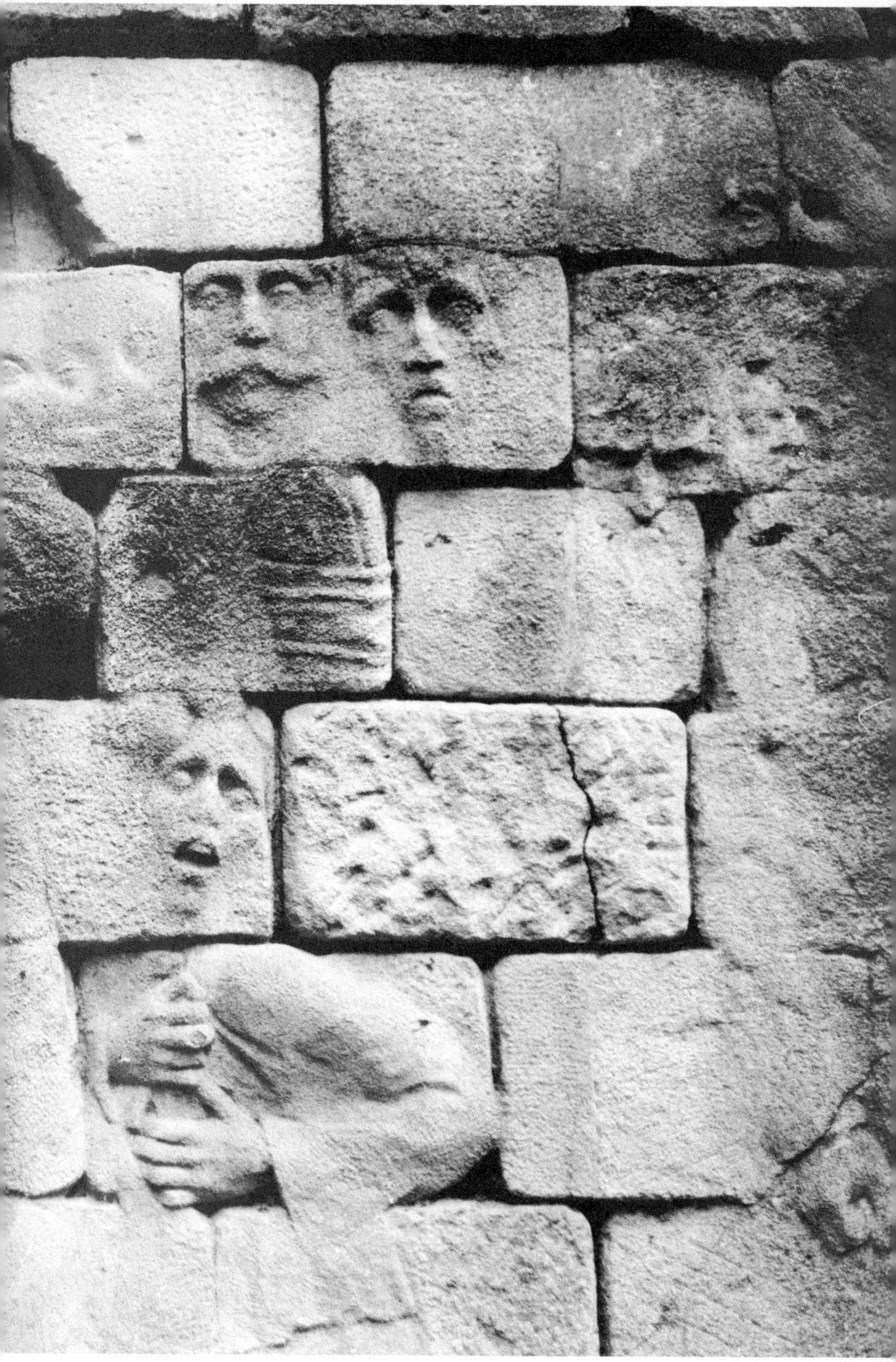

CONVERSATION WITH CARMEN TAFOLLA AND IRE'NE LARA SILVA

Maha Ahmed & Jim LaVilla-Havelin, interviewers

In 2013, Rosemary Catacalos was named the very first Latinx Texas Poet Laureate, a trailblazing accomplishment which created a ripple effect on Latinx writing communities across Texas. As of the publication date of this volume, six Texas Poets Laureate have followed her, from Carmen Tafolla in 2015, to ire'ne lara silva in 2023. As editors, we were interested in interviewing Carmen and ire'ne to understand how Rose's example and her role as a treasured member across Latinx writing communities influenced their own terms as Texas Poets Laureate. This conversation took place on Zoom on August 11, 2024.—Eds.

Maha: When did you first encounter Rosemary's work? What made it stand out?

Carmen: I don't have an exact date. It had to have been between 1977 and 1978. She read at a poetry reading with many Chicano poets of the time. Afterwards, the group went out someplace. What I remember most about the evening was that her poetry had a precision. It had a polish to it. It stood out. At that time, a lot of our stuff was very oral. Hers was, too, but it had the studied polish of discipline. You knew that it had been through many drafts. It had both the ring of oral, theatrical poetry and the discipline, depth, and precision of something that has been studied on paper. She had the ability to do both. That stood out for me the very first time I heard her read. And what stood out for me, too, was her laugh—that incredible joy. She just had a gusto to drink it all in and I don't think she ever lost that.

There were difficult times that came later, even before she got cancer. And I remember how once she said, "Carmen, I need to take two bottles of wine over to your house, and we need to drink late into the night, and it has to be on a weekend, because we're going to have to finish both of those bottles." We never did that. Both of us were busy, and shortly after that, she was diagnosed with cancer and had to be more careful about what she drank and ate. But even in the middle of that, something in her voice rang the same as her laughter on that first night that I met her. There was a gusto. There was a way of heading straight into a problem, charging into it, and either fixing it or figuring out the way to shuck it off, etc.... And for us, it was going to be that late night with two bottles of wine. As it turned out, there was still a late night or two, but without the wine.

ire'ne: I met Rosemary much, much later. I want to say it was 2004 or 2005. She was directing Gemini Ink then, and I was coordinating something for the Macondo Writers Workshop. You know how sometimes you meet certain people, and it's like you've always known them? That's what it was like. We met in her office. Talked Macondo business, and next thing I knew, we were eating tacos, talking, and dancing cumbias. I read her work after I met her, but I completely agree with everything that Carmen said. Precision is what I was thinking too. Rosa had that sort of compressed, condensed, concentrated work that I think is impossible to achieve without the technical skills and the dedication, but that also requires prioritizing truth-telling. Not just telling a true story, but telling *herself* the truth. That's what really caught me, because that kind of truth-telling as well as the compression of language and the layers of storytelling make her work work that you can read over and over again. And that's not something that can be said about every poet.

In 2016, Rosemary gave me a little medallita that she made herself. It's a red heart made of metal, with nails hammered all around into it. It's hung on a wide purple ribbon. It's beautiful. It reminds me of her work.

Jim: Rose became the first Latina Texas Poet Laureate, and then the dam broke. What did you all think? What did it mean to you to have that happen?

Carmen: For me, it was tremendous relief and pride and some playfulness. I remember a conversation Rose and I had. She was not the first Latina State Poet Laureate nominated. There had been at least four Latina poets nominated before her.

Also, she wasn't just the first *Latina*. She was the first *Latinx*. She was the first Latina *or* Latino, to be named as State Poet Laureate.

Earlier, I'd told her, "No, you try it, because your last name is Catacalos, and they'll think you're Greek. They don't realize that you're not a 100% person. You're a 200% person, you're 100% Mexican and you're 100% Greek, without any contradiction. They'll never figure out that you're Mexican."

And she said, "Well, whatever, somebody's got to get in there." So, we were joking, and this went on for about, I'd say, almost 10 years. When she was named Poet Laureate in 2012, everybody was celebrating. Everybody was super happy. We had a get together, and we have pictures from that. I think you were there, Jim. It was at the Guadalupe Cultural Arts Center's gallery.

Sometime in 2012 or 2013 there was a little get together of poets, because Rose was the State Poet Laureate, I was the City Poet Laureate, and Juan Felipe Herrera was the National Poet Laureate. And we said, in San Antonio, we have a line of *three* Mexican-Americans going up. Finally, the majority of the population of San Antonio was being represented! And we got it represented all the way! I have pictures of that. They are very happy pictures. Everybody was so celebratory. So proud. And we were especially impressed by Rose. And I remember telling her, "Rose, this is big. This is *really big*." And she said, "Nah, they still haven't figured out I'm Mexican. That's what it is."

ire'ne: Before the announcement, it really didn't seem like it was going to be possible for Latinas or Latinos to become Poet Laureate at all. So, it wasn't on my list of things to even dream about, because it seemed impossible. A lot of people might think something like this is relatively minor, but given how little poets are acknowledged, it's *major*.

When I was named Poet Laureate, I was surprised by the overwhelming amount of support and love and pride I received—and that was 10 years later. There is still such a hunger in the community to be acknowledged, to be named. To have our names go down on the official record. It's one of those times where you see the importance of *representation*. Rosa being named, and then being followed by Carmen, sent a huge wave through everyone. It made all the Latine poets, especially younger poets, think, this is possible, this is a dream we can have now.

Carmen: Yes, I underscore what ire'ne said. It did not seem like it was ever going to happen. First of all, there was a huge predominance of males. And second of all, you could go through the whole list, and there was nobody Black or brown on it. And very few women.

Jim: What does it mean to be a public poet? And how do you think Rose dealt with it and how did she help shape our consciousness of it?

Carmen: To me the State Poet Laureateship is a vehicle. It may not have wheels and it may not have gas, but it's a vehicle. Sometimes we were asked to provide the wheels and the gas, the passengers, the paint job and whatever else, but it was a vehicle that could reach so many places.

Rose, I believe, was already struggling with a cough before she was diagnosed with cancer, she was already not feeling her best, healthwise, and yet she went to the Texas Book Festival. She went to the major events. They had to get a little golf cart to drive her from one place to another at certain points but she showed up everywhere she was invited. She was always authentic about herself and about who she was. She didn't hide anything. She may have gotten in on the Greek name, but she let her Mexicanness be known. She felt courage and a sense of dedication, purpose and gleefulness about having access to this vehicle. And each one of us deals with the vehicle in her own way.

I wanted the Laureateship to be something that would allow us to take the poetry to the people. Rose did that. She was our model. And I think every single one of the people from underrepresented groups has taken that position very seriously. They understood it was not to be taken for granted, and that we have a chance. It is a vehicle, and if we have to go find wheels at a secondhand place to stick on that vehicle, to go someplace, we will. It allows us to take poetry to some unexpected places.

ire'ne: I was surprised by how much of the work of being State Poet Laureate had nothing to do with poetry. In my case, it had a lot more to do with representation. With Texas having the reputation it does, both within and outside our state, there was a great need to declare that Texas is more than its stereotypes. That there is more to Texas than negativity, prejudice, and small-mindedness. I was surprised by how many interviews I did that remarked on the unexpectedness of my being the poet to represent Texas—given that I am Latina, disabled, queer, bilingual, and so on—all these different communities I belong to. It was and continues to be so important to declare that all these communities exist *here* in Texas, that we are happy *here* in Texas, and that we have no intention of fleeing Texas and ceding it to those who don't want us here. We have families here. We have communities here. We have organizations. All these beautiful things that make our lives rich and deep and meaningful *here* and that tie us to Texas.

As Poets Laureate we have to be visible and accessible to the communities here, and make our presence known to the people outside of Texas. As the first Latina Texas State Poet Laureate, Rosa inspired that in us. How we embody the position—being who we are and coming from where we come from. The State Laureateship is a vehicle that allows for more access, so we're not just speaking to our own communities anymore. We wind up speaking to communities that wouldn't normally hear us, both within and without the state.

Maha: To tie it all back together, I'm wondering if you both could talk a little bit about how Rosemary's work influenced you as readers and writers of poetry?

Carmen: For me, what stood out with Rose was that purity of purpose. It was a search for truth, and it was painful sometimes, and it was beautiful sometimes. Her work was always deep. Every time I read her poetry, or I heard her read her poetry, or even heard her talk about poetry, it always made me want to go deeper. It made me want to dig deeper and examine deeper to get to know myself better, because I felt that's what she was doing. She was getting to know herself, via that humanity. She was getting closer to the essence of humanity by including herself in that humanness. I don't think we can ask for any bigger gift than that from a poet or from anyone. Rose made us want to be more in touch with who we are as human beings.

ire'ne: Yes! There's a poem that I dedicated to Rosa after a conversation we had. She told me that she'd had lunch with a friend, and that this friend of hers asked her what she was proudest of in her life. The friend said she imagined that Rosa was proudest of her books, her literary achievements, or her professional career.

Rosemary told her no, that that wasn't what she was proudest of, that that wasn't what poetry was in her life. Poetry wasn't about publication or acclaim—she said that poetry was what she had used in order to become the best possible version of herself.

Which led to the two of us having a whole conversation about how we as people—as spirit—move in the world, how we exist. We are fields of earth and we are the caregivers of earth. We nurture, we seed, we grow, we take care of the earth that we are, which is why that poem is called "the earth of us." It's the poetry and the attention to essence and truth and the work of it all that lets us become the best possible earth to grow and nurture a crop of some kind.

I told her that I was raised to be self-destructive. That I'd always felt it was my destiny to self-destruct and to harm as many people as possible while self-destructing. My entire goal, my entire life, has been to *not* be that. The entire point of my work is to *not self-destruct* and not cause harm in every direction.

In that conversation with Rosemary, I felt that she understood what I meant. We understood this crucial task. Poetry was not for polished publications or for awards. Poetry may include those things, but they're not the priority. When I talk to people about what self-promotion is, I tell them self-promotion is not about getting my name out there. It's not about making my bio longer or more impressive. Incidentally, publication and recognition make it possible to publish and write more, but it's about getting work out there that people need. I don't know who those people are, and I don't know where they are, but I'm doing my best to put my work within their reach. I don't know if I would have made it this far without the work of so many poets. Poetry is what helped me to not self-destruct and to dedicate myself to creating work and nurturing the creativity of others. When poetry is that in your life, it's no longer a job. It's not even a calling. It's what your *spirit* requires. It's what it demands. That's why I had to write that poem dedicated to Rosemary. We understood each other. We knew why we were poets.

the earth of us
ire'ne lara silva

for Rosemary Catacalos

"nosotras mismas somos la tierra nueva y lista para sembrar"
—Rosemary Catacalos

in the flesh of us
lavender and jasmine
and the stuff of stars

almas mias
this is the work of our lives
the black earth of us
wet with tears and sweat
and the sex of us
composted with our dreams
and our tragedies

sunlight and moonlight
limning the bone
marrow blood flesh skin of us
all our words the knives
for peeling away at
the disordered delicate
dangerous disturbed of us
until light falls unfettered
out of our eyes
the spoken the prayed
the love in the hands of us

seeds breaking open
in the revolving regenerating
rising intensity of us
and the sought for healing
stronger and stronger
streaming out of our chests
in the expanding suns of us

at our end there will be
only one essential story

what we made of the earth of us

Mr. Chairman Takes His Leave
Rosemary Catacalos

> *As to me, I know of nothing else but miracles.*
> —Walt Whitman

> *en memoria* William Rashall Sinkin, 1913-2014

Whitman, you once told me, is democracy on the page, messy
and imperfect as we are in real life, which gave you hope

that we would one day make real life true democracy, ripe blossom,
pollen dusting every moment and person, each scampering mote of light.

This is why as you lay dying, I read "I Hear America Singing"
and knew you heard every word and could feel my hand on yours

though you were already moving toward other miracles than this life.
A sunflower followed your motion and a yellow dog stood guard.

You, who lived the notion that the sun belongs to each and every one,
beggars, dreamers, kings, all. You who believed banks could have hearts,

for god's sake! You have left it to us, messy and imperfect
as we are and will be, to keep to the work side by side

and as long as it takes, all the while singing of miracles
just as Whitman and you taught us to do. Meanwhile, you

were last seen wearing blue-plaid pajamas, a contrasting
blue-plaid bow tie, and surrounded by hummingbirds.

Hummingbirds leave Texas in early February, migrating north
to make new lives. The angle of the sun tells them precisely when

to take their leave. They arrive thousands of miles away
in mid-May, about the time of your birthday. A sunflower

follows your motion. The yellow dog stands guard.

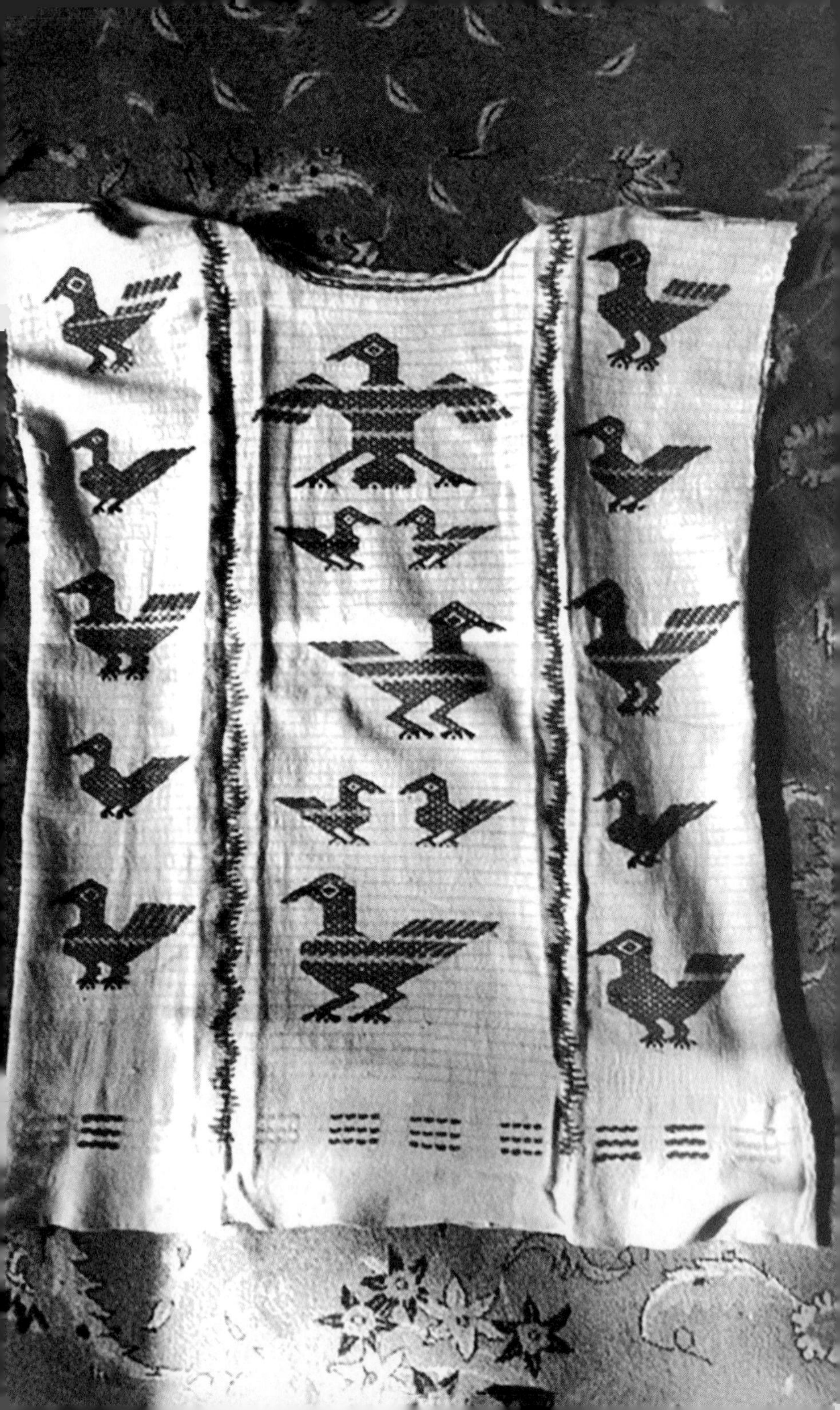

ON ROSEMARY CATACALOS'S BOOK *AGAIN FOR THE FIRST TIME*

Reginald Gibbons

Re-reading the poems of Rosemary Catacalos always seems to me as though I were reading them "Again for the First Time." The indelible emotional perceptiveness and compassion in her work are a treasure, and likewise the micro-narratives that she embeds—with just a few lines, sometimes—in some of her poems. And it was in her nature to describe or present many forms of engagement and compassion. This poet was a very devoted friend to many, and those many (myself included) were deeply graced by her spirit, her poems, her friendship, and her many generous ways of helping other poets.

In her poems she often offers us—as a gift—the opportunity to be moved, alongside her, by what she herself articulates. Her poems in *Again for the First Time* continue to grip me as if with her own hand, as if I were standing behind her, following, attending to what was happening in the poem, and as if I were seeing what she saw—a deeply companionable openness to others. At or near the center of her concerns, and her perceptiveness, was also a sense of the sheer energy—for those who are lucky enough to have it in them—for survival, for generosity to others, for her own strong self.

Her poetic narratives (or portraits or portrayals) are utterly remarkable, beginning with the poem "Katacalos," a portrait of "The Old Man," an immigrant from the Turko-Greek realm (if I can call it that), a wanderer in America, and evidently a man keenly attentive to others who had also come to the U.S. This poem takes a surprising and yet perfectly appropriate turn when, just before the last four lines, Rosemary Catacalos, having already described "The Old Man" as inadequately helpful to his wife, and also acknowledging the frustration of the wife, shows us the minute care with which the husband "just listened patiently [to his wife's complaints about getting by] / and went about setting out his / sugar water in bottle caps / to feed the ants." Not only to acquaintances and friends, but even to the ants, he provided fellow-feeling and perhaps material support!

Rosemary Catacalos often mentions food and drink, implying both everyone's need for these, and the pleasure of them. Vegetables, meat, fruit, drink. Her swift portraits of persons with few material resources show their inner resources, which seem more profound to those of us who do not have to worry about when the next meal or drink or problem will come our way. Through the poems, we see others barely making it, but nevertheless offering attentiveness and sympathy. This poet knows that there are always, along with material hardships, disappointments, and physical and emotional suffering, and death: the Dog Man, the waitress at the White House Café, "old men in khakis / left over from Villa's days," "stones of the unknown dead."

Most of us live in a populated world in which most others can be seen, can be known, but Rosemary Catacalos notices those who are not seen, those who are not known, or not yet known except as she portrays them in her poems—the poem of the ice-house man—

"Learning Endurance from Lupe at the J&A Ice House"; "And the stones of the unknown dead"; and "Señora Degollado [*degollado* is not only a Spanish surname, here, but also literally means "with throat cut"!], who complains that her tomatoes will rot / if one more drop of rain falls," and others.

It's almost impossible to grasp the enormous richness of everyday hard life that Rosemary Catacalos brings into our awareness of others, writing with such attentive sympathy about the way life is. Many of her poems celebrate hard-won survival, and the dignity of survival, and also the complex nature of persons, their celebration and their sorrow and their solace, and of what may be ordinary or humble and at the same time priceless in peoples' lives and loves, hardships and kinships. In her poems, physical and spiritual survival require, and also invite, a kind of emotional inventiveness. The pleasure of small triumphs can crown, for a day, the austerity of life's difficulties. Catacalos ends her poem "Listen, *Querido*..." with these three lines: "As thought we had not had years of practice / with holding our hearts in the fire / and at the last minute snatching them back."

I think this line (in "Blood Wedding Trilogy") is one of the most moving that I've ever read: "I come to know that death, / like birth, is a woman I can trust, / and still I am afraid." And in this poem she arrives, near the end, with a counterpoint: "The sweet, brief honeymoon underground / before bone and nail and hair are diffused / and settle into the sky for the long haul."

Toward the end of *Again for the First Time*, Catacalos presents poems that speak from a position of having inhabited myth and folklore: Ariadne, Demeter, Odysseus, and La Llorona (a folkloric Mexican ghost who in the night flies over lakes and rivers and ponds, moaning loudly because in a rage she has killed her own children after her husband left her).

And, in her poem "Tongue-Tied," she fully earned these autobiographical lines:

> All I have ever
> been trying to do is speak. It's just that sometimes
> I'm an angel
> with far too many names.... The names the others
> have given me.
> Our Lady of the Miraculous Hands.
> Our Lady of the Tainted Corners of Time.
> Our Lady of the One Word We All Know But
>   Cannot Say.
> Mother of the Ferocious Teeth.
> Mother of the Six Seeds of Spring.
> Mother of Hearts Waiting By the Sides of All Roads.
> Ariadne of the Treacherous Thread.
> Ophelia Who Died for Our Sins.
> Phoenix.
> Venus.
> Even just plain Demeter's daughter.
> I have answered
> to all these names and more.

Indeed, she has. Indeed, she did. This remarkable catalogue hints at the range of Rosemary Catacalos' beautiful, and for me, unforgettable, *Again for the First Time*. We, her readers, will always note in this book, even after several re-readings, the compassionate mastery of her attention to others—again and again, as if for the first time. Naomi Shihab Nye has written of Rosemary Catacalos in the preface of this book of poems, "She has been a tireless advocate for literacy, creative education, undersung and underheard voices. And here we were, all this time, needing hers." Needing indeed—I can think of no other work like Catacalos', and no soul larger than hers. She saw and saw into everyone whom she has portrayed in these poems. And these poems have given us her precious sense and insight, and have voiced all that she has perceived and felt so deeply.

AFTERWORD TO THE THIRTIETH ANNIVERSARY EDITION

Arthur Sze

I.

In 1983, on behalf of Tooth of Time Books, I solicited a manuscript from Rosemary Catacalos. At first she wasn't sure she was ready; she wasn't sure she had enough poems for a book. Luckily she consulted Naomi Shihab Nye. Naomi went over to Rosemary's house and helped her assemble a manuscript. When I received it, I read it with excitement and passed it along to John Brandi, the editor of Tooth of Time. John was equally excited and published *Again for the First Time* in 1984.

Thirty years later, with the first edition long out of print, it's wonderful to see that Wings Press is reissuing this collection. In rereading the poems, I'm struck by the rhythmic pulse behind each line. Rosemary Catacalos braids her dual heritage as a Mexican and Greek descendant, and she sifts through daily experience to find the mythic and timeless. At the J & A Ice House, for instance, Lupe dials a string of numbers on the pay phone and is calling somewhere very far away, only to listen, hang up, and retrieve his coin. This simple act, repeated again and again, is the book's through-line: he is always on the threshold of discovery, and it is always the first occasion. Later in the book, in the pained voice of Ariadne, the speaker notes, "these words that must be spoken." These are poems driven by necessity, and they are as alive now as thirty years ago.

As the 2013 Poet Laureate of Texas, Rosemary Catacalos will be a great ambassador for poetry, and it is important that her own work be available to readers. Bryce Milligan is to be congratulated for reissuing *Again For the First Time*. And it is my pleasure to read these poems and to discover their splendor, again for the first time.

—April 2013

II.
"Learning Endurance from Lupe at the J & A Ice House" is a poem central to Rosemary Catacalos's book, *Again for the First Time*. It begins with an epigraph from Richard Hugo:

> *Believe you and I sing tiny and wise and could if we had to eat stone and go on.*

These two lines are the ending to Hugo's poem "Glen Uig"; they are the epigraph to his collected poems, and they are the lines cut into his gravestone. As Hugo was often a poet of place, and as these lines assert strength even in death, they serve as an important foundation for Rosemary's poem where place, memory, and fortitude play such important roles.

In a narrative set in the J & A Ice House, no one knows how Lupe, "dim for a long long time," got that way, but the violence of El Salvador hangs in the air. Rosemary Catacalos's description of the violence is detailed and crisp—"charred bits of his sister's schoolbooks / and a father's crumpled tin lunchbox / were all that was left / after the soldiers had gone"—and when the speaker turns to Lupe and asks "what are we to do," the answer that is not a direct answer resides in Lupe trying to find connection, trying to find a way back. When Lupe dials on the phone and listens "for a long time until something / tells him to smile," I am reminded of Camus's existentialist essay on Sisyphus and how Camus finds that, in the midst of what appears to be a bleak, depressing and endlessly repetitive task of rolling a boulder up a hill, watching it roll down, and rolling the boulder back up, Sisyphus is not tortured but *happy*. The fleeting smile that passes across Lupe's face may be brief, but it is a redemptive moment that affirms the power to eat stone and go on. And it reminds us we need the words of those who are gone to help sustain us on our own journeys.

POEMS NEW AND OLD FROM TEXAS POET LAUREATE ROSEMARY CATACALOS

Anis Shivani

2013 Texas Poet Laureate Rosemary Catacalos, a longtime San Antonio resident of Mexican and Greek heritage, makes frequent use of the Ariadne myth in her 1984 book, *Again for the First Time*, originally published in 1984 and recently reissued by San Antonio's Wings Press in a 30th-anniversary edition. This seems a helpful entry point into Catacalos' multi-layered, enigmatic, tense work, which constructs various models of femininity and attachment only to quickly eradicate them. The same sensibility of provisionality and revision is evident in Catacalos' lovely new chapbook, *Begin Here*—also issued by Wings Press in 2013—which contains only 10 new poems but has the weight and feel of a much longer work of great complexity.

Ariadne was famously abandoned by Theseus—whom she had helped to escape from the Minotaur's labyrinth with the help of her thread—on the island of Naxos, from which she was rescued by the god Dionysus, who promptly fell in love and married her. In Greek mythology, the ideal of femininity is often embodied in the endlessly patient helpmate, though her sacrifice generally results in no great exaltation for the woman. There are few instances of women in ancient mythology who see their perseverance rewarded, and variant interpretations of Ariadne's fate cast doubt on whether Dionysus really married her at all.

In "Ariadne Seven Years Later," from *Again for the First Time*, Catacalos seeks to imagine Ariadne's condition as she waits abandoned on Naxos, and hers is a plaintive cry to Theseus against the patriarchal presumption that the suffering of women amounts to less than that of men: "Even now / when he [the Minotaur] gores me deep, decorating his wedding crown / with my blood. Even now when he tries to root out / my heart, that imperfect chalice, and offer it back / to my father in some kind of unholy tribute." Patriarchy, manifest in the male hero who takes precedence in narratives of effort and accomplishment, is inescapable, and Catacalos gives voice to female abandonment in many different registers.

In many of Catacalos' poems, women's labor is deconstructed in ways that give it a spiritual quality, thereby saving it from anonymity and grief. In "Again Ariadne," Catacalos writes about the heroine's thread: "To make / this love I give / a fit cloth for the world, / something to wear proudly." This spiritual infusion is all the more resonant in light of the modern meaning of "Ariadne's thread": the exploration of all possible logical paths toward the solution of a problem.

Similarly, in "Demeter Speaks After a Long Silence," the goddess associated with harvest addresses the gardener in terms that overturn the relationship of dependency and mastery between god and human, crediting the gardener with bringing her "these words / I had almost forgotten, / this life that had almost stopped."

Catacalos' work is informed by mythology in ways that seem at odds with standard poetic practice today. These influences operate not as inert showpieces, but as live observations on the nature of time and mortality, emphasizing the spiritual ecstasy inherent in ordinary experience. Indeed, in "Museum Piece," Catacalos turns an encounter with the poet Kenneth Koch in Galveston into a meditation on the timelessness of "the famous Greek light."

The poems in *Begin Here* typically consist of much longer lines than those in *Again for the First Time*, and their sensibility is not the classical thesis/antithesis/synthesis performance, but a more desperate descent into the abysses of irresolvable memory and nostalgia.

In "Memory in the Makings: A Poetics" (addressed to poet Lorna Dee Cervantes), Catacalos ruminates on the relentless connectivity experienced by children of the internet age, and what happens to the memory of solid relationships and work in such a condition: "And here we are on the purple lip of the cañon, telling and telling, and // there's no such thing as going too near the sun."

Where the chapbook's lines are shorter, as in "Double-fractured Sonnets from Subway and Ferry" (one of her best poems), the relative ease of movement makes us think twice as hard about the background presence of the maze, which is always present in Catacalos' poetry, as in "The eerie shine // of subway rails, Guillaume's bandaged head / bobbing in the next car to boom-box jazz," and the poem's concluding thought that "The labyrinth needs grout." There's a constant tension in this poem between the swiftness of lines such as "Beatriz is my mother's name, sweet dear / wheel of the unspoken turning a deaf ear" and the ever-present gravity of being moored in one's historical reality, signified in lines like "Pulque thick and cloudy as / night on that ferry when we were gagged and robbed // on the way to our own christening."

In "Red Dirt, Atascosa County, Texas," the imposition of daily labor is transported to the stark Texas landscape, with the ultimate reward being perhaps the recollection of labor itself: "If years / later you buy red boots and set out to find the grandfather's favorite tree, ancient / broad liveoak standing alone in the middle of the widest field in all sixteen / acres meant to save us."

Perhaps no other poem summarizes Catacalos' sensibility better than the excellent "David Talamántez on the Last Day of Second Grade," wherein the young student is marked down for every deviation from correct behavior, only to cross "out the teacher's red numbers and... [write] in huge letters, / blue ink, Yes! David, yes!" Enforced passivity is here applied to children instead of women, but the argument for spiritual escape is the same.

I'm glad to have discovered this complex poet, who, to our good fortune, has at last found a stage—Poet Laureate of Texas—large enough for her ambitions. She has tremendous skill in bringing mythical resonance down to earth, and in imbuing the landscapes she describes with a heroism that subtly counters patriarchal divisions between male protagonists and all the others. Her work will last.

Learning Endurance From Lupe at the J & A Ice House
Rosemary Catacalos

> *Believe you and I sing tiny and the wise*
> *and could if we had to eat stone and go on.*
> —Richard Hugo

When you talk to Lupe about El Salvador
his head that's too big for his body comes
slowly up off the splintered green table
at the ice house where he sweeps up every day
in exchange for a few beers. El Salvador.
He looks you straight and solemnly in the the eye
and waves one bony brown hand down the street
toward Our Lady of Sorrows.
Then with a quick flying sign of thumb
and little finger he asks for another beer
and grins.
Now Lupe has been operating on what some people
call dim for a long long time. Nobody can
even remember how he got that way or if
he was born that way or what.
But I'm here to say that he's a man
to talk to when you feel like if you tried
to plant a flower it would just die
or that if you tried to scream nothing
but flat silent air would come out.

Lupe. Los niños vieron todo, Lupe.
Even in the dark the children saw it all.
They heard it all.

How the quiet night went red with their mothers' screams.
How loved ones who moments before had been
tangled in their bedclothes
were now tangled in their common blood
and the caliche of the poverty-soaked street.
How you could only tell your brother
by the saint's medal around his neck
since all that he had dreamed with
was blasted away.
How charred bits of a sister's schoolbooks
and a father's crumpled tin lunchbox
were all that was left
after the soldiers had gone
taking with them the man who had worn
a bag for a mask
and from that doubly dark cave
had pointed out the chosen houses.
Lupe, Lupe, what are we to do
when everywhere God is committing suicide
and every one of us is God?

Lupe sways onto his feet and moves
like a dirge to the pay phone
at one end of the open shed.
He pulls the only coin
I have ever known him to have
from a stained khaki pocket,
drops it lovingly into the slot

and begins to dial and dial and dial and dial:
sixteen numbers, forty-seven numbers,
fifty numbers, all one big number. He is
calling and calling somewhere very far away.
Finally he stops and listens intently
for a long time until something
tells him to smile.
When he hangs up, his worn coin
comes tumbling back out. No charge.
Then he gives me a slow heavy nod
and he says, *Eyyy-hhhh. Eyyy-hhhhh.*
Ni-ños bo-ni-tos. Bo-o-ni-tos.
And he picks up an old broom
and goes back to work.

ROSEMARY: POET OF THE WORLD

Maha Ahmed

> *The poet in our time . . . if he does not struggle against war and oppression, he will negate whatever his words may say, and will soon have no world to say them in.* —Denise Levertov, *The Poet in the World*

During one of my first graduate classes, I introduced my work as being invested in the project of "love." I did not yet know in what way I meant this or how I would go about accomplishing it. I do know I spent the summer healing a relationship with my mother, and I'd spent four years prior studying neocolonial melancholies and deep state failure as an International Studies student. On my bad days, I believed poetry to be *extra*, an arm of solace, shiftless pocket-matter. On my good days, I let myself believe in its consequential power to change hearts, an active etching into a collective consciousness. The utility, or lack thereof, of poetry is an age-old question. From Plato's *Symposium* and Aristotle's *Poetics*, to Adorno's invocation that to write poetry after Auschwitz was barbaric, bringing to mind Nikki Giovanni's poem "For Saundra," which ends: "perhaps these are not poetic / times / at all." We continue to probe the efficacy of the lyric.

To read Rosemary Catacalos's work is to deeply involve oneself in this question, allowing the entanglements of one's "self" to mix with the peculiarities of an "other." Rosemary understood poetry as an ongoing question of humanity, of who possesses it, of how to make noumena out of incomprehensible violence. "His name and age and favorite music have bobbed away just out of everyone's reach / and he is tangled in the roots of a kindly tree," writes Rosemary about "the latest manchild found dead in Atlanta" ("A Warning from Forever"). With a chilling alacrity, we are given a precise set of facts to morally locate ourselves: the "kindly tree," a secondary victim, the ongoing criminalization of young black men, the vile endurance of lynchings, and the manufactured consent accomplished by an impartial news article. Rosemary titles the poem "A Warning from Forever," echoing afropessimism's thesis writ large, resounding Sylvia Wynter's invocation that "the negative connotations placed upon the black population group are a function of the devalorization of the *human*."

"Struggling through the work is extremely important," writes Toni Morrison, "more important to me than publishing it." Rosemary's archive reveals pages upon pages of unpublished work: notebooks filled with lecture notes, books to read, and the poems of friends with unending marginalia. Stories about Rosemary include so much of her commitment to friendship, to gathering, but most of all, to *study*. Studying, however, not by way of institution but by way of community. "I think we were committed to the idea that study is what you do with other people," writes Fred Moten in *The Undercommons*. "It's talking and walking around with other people, working, dancing, suffering...." My favorite poem of Rosemary's is

"Learning Endurance from Lupe At the J & A Ice house." Rosemary tells us of Lupe from El Salvador who "has been operating on what some people / call dim for a long long time." But Rosemary rejects this monomodal image of the man who has perhaps escaped the gruesome Salvadoran Civil War, offering his "dimness" as an invitation for political and personal resurgence:

> But I am here to say that he's a man
> to talk to when you feel like if you tried
> to plant a flower it would just die
> or that if you tried to scream nothing
> but flat silent air would come out.

During brunch at San Antonio's Liberty Bar in the summer of 2024, Rosemary's partner, Betsy Schultz, tells me that Rosemary never stopped writing, even through illness, even through treatment: "She believed in rigor." In many ways, writing is a ritual of mortality, like prayer and meditation; to write is to refuse death. "Lupe," the poem asks, "What are we to do when everywhere God is committing suicide and every one of us is God?" The poem and the incident are one; to read the poem is to be there with Rosemary, witnessing, *studying* the moment Lupe's failed attempts at a phone call "somewhere very far away" transform into a peculiar smile, a "*ni-nos bo-ni-tos*" and a return to work. We are reminded that to write is to return to work, to refuse apathy, to try, try, try.

I once believed narrative poetry to be inferior to the ephemeral avant-garde, believing performance to be poetry's apex as opposed to witness. When I first read Rosemary's work, I understood our aesthetic differences while maintaining a kinship of principle. But it was different from reading the political poets I studied during my time as an MFA student; their politics were primarily external.

Reading Rosemary felt oddly *nostalgic*. I was remembering who I was: the 13-year-old girl who wrote her first poem about some awful thing in the news, trying desperately to connect it to some other awful thing that occurred the day before somewhere else to someone else, trying, also, to tell the story of tragedy that "happens at the same time, as it's all the same world." In just a few sentences, Rosemary's poem "headscarf" contemplates Hannah Arendt's banality of evil: "the boy who goes to war because he can't think of anything else to do and his country can't either." As an Arab, I often shy away from poems that border oriental fetishism, that can turn complicated material objects, like the headscarf, into symptoms of erotic imperial projection. But I am enamored by Rosemary's delicacy with the final image:

> When he comes back he doesn't know his family, remembers nothing but the girl dead at his feet, her headscarf, O, her embroidered headscarf, its colored threads shaped into a flowering border keeping nothing out, keeping nothing in.

An image that deftly encapsulates U.S. imperialism at its core: the complex discourse of the infamous headscarf, an object levied as the symbol of female oppression, used to justify unspeakable levels of violence in the Middle East. Rosemary understood such connective threads on a cavernous level. Rosemary's lens is as wide as it needs to be, as narrow as she sees fit. There is a wisdom to her poetic choices that obviates even the most eloquent craft talk. One of the many reasons I have turned away from narrative is precisely this: the fear of getting it wrong, the fear of detail. Like most immigrant children, I fear a shrinking archive, that the minutiae of my life and the wrinkled hands of my elders will soon be made obsolete by a grander narrative masked in geopolitics and infographics. Rosemary's poetry reminds me that there is no such thing as an irrelevant detail or a story too small to tell. The opening poem in *Again for the First Time* introduces us to Rosemary's father: Katakalos, "brought up on routine whippings every Sunday," who always got "sidetracked caring for some sick bird or dog or donkey," and "braved the maze of Ellis Island / alone at sixteen / escaping with his last name intact / and his first name changed to Sam." Rosemary goes on to describe the popcorn and ice cream wagon, and his angry wife, who "hated the way he was always attracting winos and gypsies / and cousins from everywhere," spanning the love and generosity of her Greek father who couldn't achieve economic mobility "since he always told the poor kids to pay him back whenever they got the money."

The stories of immigrants are not a slush-pile of refugee trauma, but accounts of specificity, entire planets within this daily practice of exilic living: re-learning a tenderness robbed from you at every liminal border. The multiplicity of the archive is further ensconced in Rosemary's preoccupation with the Greek goddess Ariadne. A true alchemist, Rosemary churns diegeses into gracious wisdom. Ariadne a case in point, Rosemary transmutes her Greek heritage into spirit, recasting the stories of wronged women, restoring their justice in poetry: "I call up the bull and a lamb appears, / too feeble to carry the heavy horns, / much less draw the blood of love," (Ariadne III). Rosemary was a staunch feminist, and all the women in her poems have somewhere important to go, something thrilling to say, comfortable in their erotic and divine faculty, even and especially the mothers in "La Casa" who "will go on praying / that we might be simple again."

Rosemary understands Ariadne's betrayal on a symbiotic level, that she is not simply an abandoned relic of Theseus's victory, but a deep and uncompromising lover of all things, a woman who understands both her power and how it has been taken advantage of—her kindness mistaken for naïveté. She imagines her new life with Dionysus not as a clean victory but a precarious second chance:

> Sometimes I'm still afraid. You know that.
> I am, even if a princess, a simple weaver
> of spells. Sometimes of faith that
> there will be no more mazes, no more beasts.

Above all, I am most obsessed with Rosemary's obsession with her friends. "There can be no politics without collectivity," writes Gayatri Spivak. So many of her poems have epigraphs dedicated to someone—sometimes anonymous, sometimes not—with the earnestness of a second person "you" pulsing in and out of the poem. Where there is a void in justifying poetry's *raison d'etre*, Rosemary replaces it with a friend. Where she cannot write *for* something, she writes *to* someone, offering grace, comfort, a plaintive hope in hours of discomfort. "Sleep, little sister," she writes to her dear friend Naomi Shihab Nye, "Soon the morning will open / again in the simple sighing of roses."

It is, of course, unsurprising to hear that Rosemary was a stubborn and persistent person, dedicated mostly to *the work* in all its forms. It is unsurprising to hear how seriously she took the job of Poet Laureate—traveling to multiple schools and putting on programming around the city, how she understood poetry as a vehicle for soul-purification as opposed to fame, how she balances iterations of worldliness and universality with political realities, each poem a fresh attempt at care.

Rosemary's work is not simple *about* insistence but *is* insistence itself. To read Rosemary in this hour is to engage in an affirmation of the preciousness of life. As multiple neo-imperial forces work to annihilate Palestine, it is poets like Rosemary who remind us that there is no such thing as an anonymous human being. Rosemary, in her dedication to specificity, in her unremitting mourning and remembrance of her dear friends, reminds us that it is imperative to remember one another, to record what we can, to be one another's witnesses and above all—to love, love, love.

Works Cited:

Harney, Stefano, and Fred Moten. *The Undercommons : Fugitive Planning & Black Study*. Minor Compositions, 2013.

Giovanni, Nikki. "For Saundra," *Voetica*. https://voetica.com/poem/10643.

Spivak, Gayatri Chakravorty. *Death of a Discipline*. Columbia University Press, 2003.

"The Art of Fiction No. 134." *The Paris Review*, 17 Jan. 2023, www.theparisreview.org/interviews/1888/the-art-of-fiction-no-134-toni-morrison.

Wynter, Syliva, et al. "On How We Mistook the Map for the Territory, and Reimprisoned Ourselves In Our Unbearable Wrongness Of Being, Of Desêtre: Black Studies Toward the Human Project (2005)." *I Am Because We Are*, REV-Revised, 2, University of Massachusetts Press, 2016, p. 116.

"and where are the women poets?"
—a reply

Rosemary Catacalos

this woman is no moon;
what you see, she owns
and more;
pain, fruit, visions
push between her legs
into the mexican streets,
into office building mail slots,
into musicians' beds
and political strategy meetings;
she piles them on altars,
fills her daily coffin with them,
celebrates easter
at every opportunity
with candles, bread, red eggs;
she owns her laughter,
her incest, her grief;
owns portions of her compassion,
of all the hands she's ever held,
of all the vagabonds, tramps,
magicians, gypsies, jokers,
wanderers, all the blessed
who ever sought the garden;
owns constantly, every second,
over breakfast, in the car,
at the ocean, through the windows,
in the music, with the madmen,
in the churches,

at the desk,
at the well,
the wonder at why blood isn't blue,
a color to ward off the evil eye;
owns the mirror, owns the labor
owns the fever,
the pain of labor
the ecstasy at bearing illusion,
the necessary child
still, men stop her in the street
to pummel her womb and ask angrily
why she will not give birth.

[Finally the best things are simple]
Rosemary Catacalos

Finally, the best thing are simple, trust
themselves. Trees on the river throw armfuls
of grackles into the air

of grackles up in the air

Finally, the best things are simple, trust
themselves and us with them. River trees

Finally, the best things are simply, trust
themselves and us with them. Riverbank trees
throw armfuls of grackles into the air

The Lesson in "A Waltz for Debby"
Rosemary Catacalos

> *in memory of Bill Evans*

Amazing how this world manages to be all of a piece.
In Beirut an old woman hearing guns that are nothing
like drums pulls her apron up over her head
and wrings the air in entreaty. In La Ressurecion,
Guatemala, Mayan Indians in bright handmade cloth
are hung in the trees with their wrists slit and
left to die slowly, turning like obscene ornaments

or jungle birds. And on a strait named Juan de Fuca
the coast of Washington State, a stranger
is within peaceful shouting distance of six whales
rising and falling on the water: the usual

and regular breathing of God. All this has everything
to do with how you wrote "Waltz for Debby" when she
was three and still had a right to believe life
would always come in gentle measures, the swoop and
sweep of a good dream doing what comes naturally.
You knew better but went ahead

anyway. Just as today I balanced in sunlight
with my own three-year-old nieces, clambering the distance
around one of Fuller's dreams become a toy, the joyful
geometry of a dome marked off into triple-sided air.
Even if Demetra refused to step where her favorite tree
cast shadows and twice wouldn't pronounce
the name of her missing uncle,
suspecting the pain it would bring out in the open.

Later she was sullen with the weight of it. Her swing
would not fly, though she leaned with all her might
and crazily against gravity. I thought how all the waltzes
in the world wouldn't save her from learning this.

The man watching the whales, meanwhile, may
fear that in a few years there won't be whales
on this coast. Or men either, for that matter.
But also he remembers your fingers as wingtips,
your remains as clear notes
phrased with possibility. And since jazz musicians
mostly work nights, how you were always finding
your way in the dark.

Women Series I
Rosemary Catacalos

the rain bed, a place
for celebration,
every drop a memory of
blood flowing between
the legs of centuries,
of Isis in lazuli blue,
of brown mothers
   tenderly lavishing
   the gift of speech,
of apple-cheeked peasant
   women warming their
   love in frozen fields;
having cut off the
child's hand so
she will be a good beggar,
having married her
son in a summerhouse
having been your mother,
wife, lover, killer,
        savior,
        courier,
     prayer,
     liar,
     seer,
        judge and bearer
from the scarlet letter
to the easter stone,
into it all she whispers,
"creation, creation.
and the fact
that i know."

Sight Unseen
Rosemary Catacalos

Homenaje a Rosario Castellanos

Rosario did not live long into our digital age and certainly never saw or
dreamed screens in every hand, much less flooding every head. Already

it was bad enough, she said, that telenovelas in her beloved México
had displaced both Homer and Scheherazade, not to mention the days

when people gathered simply to listen to fire. A neighbor brings the last
of his garden's kale, which I take to a ninety-eight-year-old friend

whose eyes well up at the thought of strong kale soup and how very kind
most people are. A woman who sets the example of at least one mitzvah

every day, what she calls the absolute minimum for anyone human.
My neighbor, the one with the kale, is the son of a double immigrant.

His father was a Catalán who decamped to France—guess when—
and later northern California. I've wondered if this man was among

the huge crowds that survivors of the Abe Lincoln Brigade
attracted in Berkeley well into the late nineties. Delmer Berg,

last of the twenty-eight hundred Lincolns, died in San Francisco,
February 2016, one-hundred-and-one years old. Today a gardener

raises index and middle finger in front of his eyes, a sign for "Let's
look at it." We are both speaking Spanish, but his thinking is it never

hurts to repeat, whatever the case. See what I'm saying?
The Mexican women in my family see beyond the usual senses.

Always have done. My Yucatán Maya-Spanish grandma asking ¿Qué te pasa?
when clearly she already knew. Whatever it was. This year on her birthday,

thirty-five years after her death, a calla dormant in my garden for seven years
sends up a tiny bud that blooms days later on her elder daughter's birthday.

That daughter, my mother. The calla, my mother's favorite. Last year we
buried Mami in a basket under dozens of callas tied with hand-woven Mexican

belts. See what I'm saying? I don't know if the Greek women in my family
have second sight because I don't know them. But I do know a second cousin

I've never met searched the internet for kin of her grandmother Amirza's
little brother who left their island for America at fourteen, never to be seen

by his family again. This cousin found me via a TV documentary where I
recount the confusions of a mixed-blood descendant of the Mexican revolution.

María Zouni Tsimourtos was born on Imbros, but the family left when
the Turkish government took the last Greek farms in 1964. Our great-

grandmother, mother of Amirza and my grandpa, was named Sultana,
commonly a Turkish name. And here am I, a mestiza's mestiza who wept

only one of the many times I've been called half-breed. I know irony like a
second skin, haphazard skein of blood weaving a cloak of many stories

and tongues. My neighbor, the one who grows kale, spoke French as a
first language, not Spanish. Because his father was raised speaking Catalán,

not Spanish, then wisely favored French safety just across the border
and later put his son in San Francisco's French American Bilingual School.

Oh, do see this world chasing its million and one tales, sight unseen,
all language common mistranslation yet most precious lost and found.

Outcast
Rosemary Catacalos

Today, the first of your going,
I wore my yellow dress
and tried to walk into the river
to repeat the miracle of baptism.
But I couldn't get past the grasses
I got tangled on the bank.
The river rushed away hissing,
"You can't expect to come back here.
This is no longer your bed."

The second day.
The second sin of too much trying.
I remember that once when I left you
alone in this town you asked,
"And if I see them flying . . . ?"
I circled Main Plaza,
grabbing the old men by the shoulders.
Baring my breasts, I begged them
to carry me up into the healing air.
But they wouldn't even wave.
They wouldn't even talk about old times.
Many were disgusted and pulled their
sweat-stained hats down over their faces.
Others crossed themselves with their eyes closed
and then sat on their hand.
The kindliest among them whispered,
"It is your need, your fever,
your incompleteness we don't like.
How weakly you remember grace.
No, m'ija. La vida es muy corta.
Life is too short to squander our soaring

on something not quite lover, not quite angel."
Across the street in the cathedral
The Virgin turned her back on me again.
It started to rain,
but the drops refused to touch me.
Even my tears rolled off fast,
not wanting to be seen with me.
I have been everywhere,
right down to the trash piled
outside your empty apartment.
All over town doors are slamming,
making my ears bleed.
I can't even get drunk.
Nothing will embrace this shameful ghost
dragging the weight of its gravestone
around to all its old haunts.

Headscarf
Rosemary Catacalos

This world so heavy with sadness. The daughter who asks her father please not to die in winter, please, as winter is so dark. Or the neurosurgeon who has a stroke and now drags his left leg around, "does yards," and eats only every other day. All this happens at the same time, as it's all the same world. The boy who goes to war because he can't think of anything else to do and his country can't either. When he comes back he doesn't know his family, remembers nothing but the girl dead at his feet, her headscarf, O, her embroidered headscarf, its colored threads shaped into a flowering border keeping nothing out, keeping nothing in.

Question to the Master on the Ways of Synchronicity
Rosemary Catacalos

> *When everything happens at once, no conflicts can occur.*
> —Hayden Carruth

Master, yesterday in Chinatown my eyes kept leaving
      the teeming streets, wizened faces and piles of trinkets,
to rise toward the balconies floating there bright
      and intricate as the undersides of chrysanthemums.
How at ease with the thousands of years must one be
      to lean a wet string mop over a railing of gilded dragons,
how precisely trusting? As at dusk I stood shifting
      my weight in the chill, listening to an old jazz man
do Mingus in a doorway, how he said he's forgotten the names
      of the notes, now just plays the music. And up it went,
that music, alongside dense smells of herbs and incense,
      keeping the beat with the air until I swear
I heard huge wings beating too. As if from every shop and alley
      ancient cranes, silk, jade, paper, bone, were rising toward
the kind of memory that promises just the right timing.
      My friend Sze says the Chinese ideogram for *tree* can mean
many things at the same time. Tell me, then, will two trees
      take the shape of a boundless forest: simultaneous light
and shadow becoming a thousand doorways, all opening
      into the world, all opening out?

ON COLLABORATING WITH ROSEMARY

Cary Clack

I resisted collaborating with Rosemary Catacalos on the poem which would be "Resistance: A Protocol."

The idea was absurd. Had I suggested it, the idea would have been especially absurd. Rosemary suggested it and it was still absurd.

I'm not a poet. Rosemary was a brilliant and widely acclaimed poet and the former Poet Laureate of Texas.

Spurring her suggestion was an idea of Jim LaVilla-Havelin's, the *San Antonio Express-News* poetry editor, to use National Poetry Month of 2017 to honor poets and their readers with what he called a "poetic conversation between poets Bryce Milligan, Sheila Black, Carmen Tafolla, Naomi Shihab Nye, Rosemary Catacalos, Cary Clack and Juan Felipe Herrera. They were asked to respond to each other's work."

Some of you observant readers may be looking at that list and saying to yourself, "What an interesting collection of poets to have—Wait!—Cary Clack's not a poet."

Didn't I already say that myself? And not only was I the only one of those listed who wasn't a poet, my name was right next to Herrera who was, at the time, the U.S. Poet Laureate.

Yes, I resisted, but Rosemary was a big sister-like good friend who had more faith in me than I did, she talked me into it, saying it would be fun.

And it was.

Rosemary would email me a line and I'd respond by riffing off it and then she'd riff off what I sent. We flowed effortlessly. As I said before reading it at her memorial service in 2022, I don't remember whether some lines were hers or mine. That they were *ours* makes me proud.

Revisiting that time and rereading our poem reminds me how much I miss her and her voice.

On Mother's Day, 2022, Rosemary called me one last time to say she was transitioning. She apologized for making my day heavy, but I told her I was fine because I could feel she was at peace.

Then, she said, "I love this world. I love this world so much, despite all of its problems."

And we loved Rosemary because she made the world lovelier with her presence despite its problems.

In 2013, at the memorial service of her former father-in-law, Bill Sinkin (a visionary businessman and advocate for social justice) Rose read her poem "Mr. Chairman Takes His Leave." It's a tribute to Sinkin, his faith in democracy and devotion to making its promise true for all:

> You have left it to us, messy and imperfect
> as we are and will be, to keep to the work side by side
> and as long as it takes, all the while singing of miracles
> just as Whitman and you taught us to do.

Our messy and imperfect democracy no longer has the pleasure to count Rosemary as one of its citizens. But she's left us psalms of hope so that we will find the miracles we can sing.

Resistance: A Protocol
Rosemary Catacalos and Cary Clack

Our job now is to inhabit the logic
of song, feed our native soil as
it opens to receive seed; learn other,
not "foreign," languages. We

insist to persist to resist in songs accented by histories and tilled in grace. Plains fruited by the strange and familiar echo of the blues and resurrected harmonies

study where we fall on the bell
curve of being, call safety on the dark
country road at night. Our job now
is to learn how the shapes of birds

shape ancient destinies, emerging emboldened from sanctuaries, eyries, nests of grace-amazing, eyes on prizes foretold and self-evident

defining magnificent flight in song
and summoning "the condition of music"
to release our most sacred words:
trust, love, justice. Hermana, adelfí,

sweet honey bleeds from rocks, marking guideposts for mockingbirds, who, gifted with the world's tongues see they've passed here before and know how to proceed.

Brother, adelfós, the hard-work dance
begins time and again with hard music.
But with each step the circle grows
and turns without fail into the light!

Art as an Act of Agression, or See Dick Run

He says his name is Dick, which I can only assume to be a pseudonym, and a most unoriginal one at that. He invades my life with telephoned obscenities one sunny summer Sunday because he hasn't learned the right kind of agression. But we'll get back to Dick.

I first visited this show with Anita Valencia about ten days ago. As I examined each piece, I was struck by the range and variety of the making we see here. It would be less than authentic of me to say that I find all of the work to be on the same level in terms of technical proficiency, overall impact, or even motivation. Technically the pieces represent everything from what I would consider to be beginning work to very sophisticiated, sharply-honed expression. Likewise, the range of impact upon me as a viewer runs from simple acknowledgment to real involvement with certain pieces. And in terms of motivation, I sense a range running from work that represents one perhaps ancillary facet of the maker's life to work done out of the kind of personal urgency that makes a fundamental and central commitment to the making of art.

What then holds the show together for me? There are some recurring themes and images that strike me as I view the show as a whole. Much of the work suggests layers, veils, borders, torn edges, the sense of breaking through and out of these boundaries, the sense of emerging, of coming out. It is a sense that pervades much of contemporary women's work in all disciplines and worldwide, for obvious historical reasons.

Also, many of the same colors show up in a variety of works. There is much delicacy and tenderness in the many pinks and blues, and these often coexist with the more emphatic purples, wines and reds. These are colors that are often associated with "women's work," but I come away with the sense that here there is often the goal of rescuing this palette from preconceived notions to renew its vitality.

Art as an Act of Agression - 2

But for me, the overwhelming common thread of the show is the fact of its
making, the fact that so many women at various levels of involvement have
chosen to make something in response to their lives, to say something
about themselves and our world. The fact that all such making, and the
impetus that leads to it, is dignified, positive, and worthy of our highest
respect.

Think of art as an act of agression, a friend said to me the other day.
On reflection, my response is that simply being alive while exercising
life-affirming consciousness and responsibility is an act of agression --
an agressive determination to stand up and be counted against the de-
structive forces that are always present in this world. In this sense,
prayer is an act of agression, and certainly the making of art.

Now back to Dick and his variety of agression. The irony is that Dick
called as a result of having seen my photograph in last Sunday's paper
along with an announcement of this talk. Thus, the work around us and
the loving spirit of making that went into it, takes on a special meaning
for me. It is an antidote to Dick's version of reality, a positive act
of agression aginst his worldview. It is a prayer for him and for the
transformation of what he represents.

Delivered as A Poet's Response to the
San Antonio Women's Caucus for Art exhibition
in conjunction with Contemporary Art Month,
San Antonio, Texas, 31 July 1987
Rosemary Catacalos

THE UNSUNG MASTERS SERIES

POETS VOICE WILL LIVE ON IN THE WORLD SHE LOVED

Cary Clack

As Rosemary Catacalos prepared for hospice, she said, "I love this world. I love this world, so much, despite all of its problems."

On Christmas Day 2019, shortly after I'd returned to the "Express-News," I received a text from Rosemary Catacalos.

"Beloved hermanito," she wrote. "I write with the greatest good wishes for you and yours in celebration of the Christmas season. Apologies for going silent a while, but I have been bound and determined not to distract you even slightly from your first week and column. I have been ill since Dec. 11. A new cancer treatment and I do not get along."

She concluded, "PLEASE don't allow this news to get in the way of your work!"

She'd sketched the character of a great friend, mentor and poet, one so selfless that she felt the need to apologize for being silent because she was being treated for cancer.

Rose, the first Latina to be named Texas Poet Laureate, died June 17 after living with cancer for more than seven years. She was 78.

Death never silences a poet's voice, not after it's been spoken and heard, never after it's been written and read, and few voices resonated like that of Rosemary Catacalos, one of the best poets this city and state has produced.

"I cannot bear the thought that her indelible voice won't be coming over the telephone anymore," poet Naomi Shihab Nye, her friend of 51 years, said. "She made so many melodic sounds or intonations as parts of regular conversations—the 'huh' and 'meh' and 'uh-huh' type.

Little more than a week before her death, two of Rose's close friends, Betsy Schultz and Bett Butler, set up a page for friends to receive updates and send messages. Butler, a magnificent jazz singer, wrote of Rose's "use of tempo, space, and breath; the judicious seasoning of Texas drawl or a Spanish phrase beautifully rendered."

It was a magnificent voice, one that initially confused me.

I first met Rose in 2003 shortly after she became executive director of Gemini Ink, the literary arts center. I knew she was of Greek and Mexican heritage and grew up speaking Spanish, Greek and English, and I heard in her voice what Naomi and Bett heard. But I also heard the voice of a Black woman.

It all made sense when I learned Rose grew up on the East Side and had imbibed the idiom of the Black community in which she lived as deeply as she'd absorbed the rhythms and nuances of the languages spoken in her household.

Her poem "Swallow Wings" begins with the lines, "I been to church, folks. I'm an East Side Meskin Greek and I been to church." The poem is dedicated to Maya Angelou, who encouraged her to speak in all her languages.

Through the years, Rose and I would talk about our experiences of growing up on the East Side, and the blessings of being the oldest grandchild and living with or near grandparents.

"She was elegant," Nye said. "Her voice in every language was gorgeously resonant. She was always wise. Beyond all of us somehow."

On Mother's Day, Rose called to tell me the cancer had spread. "I'm going to begin . . . , " there was a slight pause, "transitioning."

She apologized for making my day heavy—again with the apology—but I told her I was fine because I could feel she was at peace.

Then, she said, "I love this world. I love this world so much, despite all of its problems."

In 2013, at the memorial service of her former father-in-law, Bill Sinkin, the visionary businessman and advocate for social justice, Rose read her poem "Mr. Chairman Takes His Leave." It's a tribute to Sinkin, his faith in democracy and devotion to making its promise true for all:

"You have left it to us, messy and imperfect as we are and will be, to keep to the work side by side and as long as it takes, all the while singing of miracles just as Whitman and you taught us to do."

It's a song of hope.

Rose, you've taken leave of this world you loved, despite Ukraine, Uvalde and the unrest of insurrection. We must find the miracles we can sing. We must keep to the work, side by side.

THE ROSE CHRONICLES

Betsy Schultz

How to Fish:

Rose and I used to go fishing.

My parents owned a little house on the water in deep south Texas. I asked Rose if she would like to go down sometime. "No not really, I've been to The Valley. I'm good." For two years, more or less, we went back and forth in this manner.

Finally—I think just to shut me up—she said yes. So off we went. This trip changed everything. It was love at first sight. Over time, it became a sanctuary for her.

Later I bought the house from my mother. As often as we could we were there. We remodeled and truly made it ours.

During this time, I found our fishing guide, Roger. (Neither one of us had much of an idea how to fish, so a good guide was critical. He was the best.) There was no more enthusiastic fishing person than Rose. I think one of their best moments together was "Reel it Rose, you've hooked 10 times!"

All three of us almost fell off the boat laughing.

Whistling:

Rose could whistle. Her specialty was a single-note, one-breath, impossibly long alto whistle—always the same note.

I didn't know this about her until the day we were shopping in a big box store. We went our separate ways. Above the noise of the shoppers, I heard someone far away whistling. I wondered who could—or would—do that. And then I just knew—Rose!? I followed the whistle several aisles over and back. There she was—rather gleeful, I think. I have always wondered what the shoppers around her were thinking while she stood there alone whistling.

When she was a little girl, she liked to sit in the kitchen as her mother was cooking. She practiced her one-note whistle. Rose said her mother would get really mad at her when she wouldn't stop.

Greek Food:

We often went to John the Greek for lunch. The two families had known each other for at least a generation. She spoke in Greek to the owner. I think it meant a lot to Effie for Rose come in; they had known each other for so long. And I know it meant much to Rose to be there with them.

Lunch:

Rose and I first met in the mid-1990s through mutual friends. She was in town from California and I was just back from New York. We got to chatting at a party, and at some point, I thought we were having a good conversation so I suggested lunch. It didn't take more than a second for her to answer "No! I'm too busy."

The end.

That was our first lunch.

Skip forward a few years when word went out that Rose was moving back from California. I was skeptical; however, once again through mutual friends, we were thrown together for a monthly scheduled wine and talk. I am not sure how it began, but I think we finally decided we could take one car. This is how we got to having lunch—first squeezed into work days, eventually celebrated after retirements—lunches escalating from an hour to all afternoon.

My learning began there. Even though we always sat at the same table, Rose was not always present as her ears focused on the next table, listening to their conversations.

Hearing stories.

Gathering ideas.

In the beginning, I was hurt, angry, and frustrated that my stories were not enough. But there was no point in resisting; after some time, I had to give in. I came to understand that the listening, the storytelling—no matter the origin—was the only point.

We came together.

We both learned from each other.

Fiat:

In 2015, I bought a red Fiat sports car. That same year, Rose became Texas Poet Laureate.

I told her I would be her driver on the Laureate Tour, but only if we went in the Fiat. She said yes!

Off we went. Always running a little late getting out of town. Always taking the country roads there and back. A little lost sometimes, but always meeting and talking to people. With directives to each other back and forth:

"Stop the car! Just stop the car!!" This directive came whenever we saw old and beautiful buildings in small towns.

"Where are you going? Why are you stopping?" This came when we were driving home from Houston and the insane traffic pushed us off the freeway because any small road would be better.

"Get out of the car! Just get OUT of the car!" This came when driving through a small town and I happened to look up. Overhead were thousands of sandhill cranes on their way to the Gulf.

I thought she would never get out of the car, but she did.

A great day. In a great year. In a small red car.

Lemons:

Rose called, "Would you like to pick lemons today?" How could I say no to that? It didn't occur to me that it might be something of a trick question.

Rose had the place but needed me to climb the trees to get the lemons. She "supervised" from below. These were no tame lemons; they were grown from seeds brought from Greece by her father and planted at the San Antonio Greek American Society property built and owned by her parents.

I didn't have a chance. The thorns all over the limbs could have sewn a leather saddle, and I was scratched and impaled before I finished. The method was to pick from the ladder wedged in the limbs while looking out for thorns all around me, then throw them down onto blankets we had laid down. Most made the blanket, but a few hit the dirt and burst open.

Her parents were there enjoying the fall afternoon during all of this, watching our adventure but not saying too much. When the picking was done, we got them up and into our baskets. I found a few busted ones that had missed the blankets. It was the first time I had ever smelled a lemon fresh from the tree—and I have never smelled one quite like that since. These were big fat drippy juicy things slippery with lemon oil. I was so besotted I went over to her father to share this sweet scent. I didn't know him very well and thought my appreciation of the lemons might help me. I walked over to him, lemon in hand, and said, "You have to smell this! Amazing!" Barely looking up from where he sat, he replied, "I've smelled a lemon."

Rose and I rolled our eyes.

"I've smelled a lemon." We used that line for years.

Gotta Make My Book:

One time at the coast we had to go to our local bait shop, which really is more like a bait hardware food store city center. I do not know how they fit everything in there. I have never gone for want.

We probably needed some ice. We were a little early but the store was open. I let Rose go in while I got the ice. When Rose returned, I learned that the lady at the register was real put out because she already that morning had a conversation with a fisherman who needed his bait for the day. She was not open at that time and not going to open early just because he needed some bait. He had to wait as she needed to "make her coffee and do her book" for the day. I believe she had to repeat herself several times. Finally, she said, "you've used up 5 minutes already, now it's going to take longer."

On this same trip. We had to go into Raymondville. As we drove through town, Rose wanted to stop for a soda pop. I stayed in the car. And stayed. And stayed. What could she be doing in there? Meanwhile, I kept seeing people going in, but so few were coming out. What can she be doing? What is going on in there?

Finally, she came out. I told her: "I was thinking to check on you but you were in there so long and I didn't want to join in!"

Rose told me that the clerk had a full house and no other person on a register and a line around the tiny aisle. When her manager finally appeared, the clerk said, "They have to wait. They don't want to wait. They have to wait. I have to count my bank."

This was our Count My Book Tour.

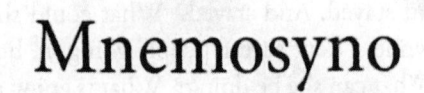

Mnemosyno

Memorial Celebration for Rosemary Catacalos

¡Gracias a la vida!

March 18, 1944 — June 17, 2022

Carver Community Cultural Center
September 9, 2022

ON MNEMOSYNO

Bett Butler & Joël Dilley

The first Latina/Greek Poet Laureate of Texas embraced the color and beauty of her multicultural upbringing in every aspect of daily life: her surroundings, the clothes she wore, the music she listened to, the words she wrote. Her passion for the arts led to countless collaborations and friendships with artists across all genres.

For this film shown at her memorial celebration, composer Joël Dilley wrote and orchestrated "Mnemosyno," inspired by her poem of the same name. Shown are images from the home she created: a view through her kitchen window; a settee upon which she was once photographed, now covered with bright pillows and multi-hued throws; a beautiful beaded tapestry; a family altar. Included are short clips from readings ranging from the University of Texas Poetry Center to San Antonio's Eastside Lockwood Park, where we see her shaking her finger at us just like the preacher lady in her poem "Swallow Wings." The film ends with a poignant reading recorded shortly before her death, "Mr. Chairman Takes His Leave."

(Her collection of beautiful and well-used hand drums and percussion instruments later found a home at Mandala Music Production, where Dilley reworked "Mnemosyno" with added tracks played live on those instruments.)

Mnemosyno
Rosemary Catacalos

in memory of Sam Sinkin

A man dies suddenly and just as suddenly a certain
wave of the hand, the rumple of a linen jacket,
the simple drumbeat of his laughter, become
crucial in a way that yesterday they were not.
Now that there will never be time for that cup
of coffee we were always going to have and that
discussion of the Bill of Rights.
Now that I'll never get to ask you about the special
way this world fit together for a man who built
a Western wear factory and read more than most
and whose mother had kept her samovar boiling and
boiling in a strange country.
Now that what you have taken with you is yours
and what each of us remembers of you is ours,
this is what you have given me to keep:
The bittersweet cries of Yaacov's accordion
at Steven Ross' wedding feast.
Your hand softly beating time on the hotel tablecloth.
The faraway look in your eyes as you watched
us dance the hora, our arms and legs waving
like an ancient line of seaweed swaying on
the floor of the Mediterranean.
The way all at once your face shone as though
you were not only seeing us, as though you
were seeing peace and hearing the world's
heart pound for joy in this dance that
Jews, Arabs, Greeks, Turks, Armenians, brothers
in time and music, all hold in common trust.

The way at that moment you *knew* something,
remembered something that had long
been lost to this earth.
It was just then that Cousin Hana called to you
from the line of dancers, jolted you back
to this celebration in this hotel in Texas.
Sam, she cried. *Sam! Come and dance!*
Everybody dance!
I remember the playful wave you gave her
and the way your eyes almost shut
with sudden laughter. And you shouted back
I am dancing! You were dancing, Sam,
and now that it's become so crucial
we see you're dancing still.

A SEAMLESSLY COMMITTED LIFE: DENISE LEVERTOV, 1923 - 1997

Rosemary Catacalos

She was so fiercely alive she could scarcely contain herself. A passionate co-conspirator with everything living: people, animals, trees, mountains, flowers, this whole little planet. She wanted it all *To Stay Alive* (the title of her ninth book of poems). Which is why it's so hard to believe that she's gone. It's as if a great river, or a wind pattern, or even a whole season, had simply stopped in its tracks and left.

Denise Levertov, internationally respected poet, powerful theorist in poetics, and committed progressive activist, died on December 20 from complications of lymphoma, less than two months after her seventy-fourth birthday. Those of us who called her friend are reeling, uncomprehending, though she had been ill for some time.

I was blessed to be among hundreds of people all over the world, many of them writers and artists, with whom Denise shared her time, her wisdom, and her love. She was my friend, mentor, sometimes even mother. It was not always clear in which order, and it didn't matter. The roles were threads of the same cloth, part of the seamless whole of her life.

As a theorist, Denise was perhaps best known as the exponent of Organic Form, based in the notion that all experiences and things have an inherent form, which it is our task as poets (as creators in any discipline) to find and reveal. Organic form, she taught, can only be exercised from a stance of "faithful attention," of "standing open-mouthed," and then being "brought to speech" before life.

Good poems are made, she said,

> when ear and eye, intellect and passion, interrelate more subtly than at other times; and the 'checking for accuracy,' for precision of language, that must take place throughout the writing is not a matter of one element supervising the others but of intuitive interaction between all the elements involved.

—from "Some Notes on Organic Form"
The Poet in the World (1960)

This was not a narrowly intellectual poetics, it was an ethic, a mode of conduct that made itself felt in all she said and did: making poems, opposing war, loving nature, all of it.

The weather has been warming for days. An early March evening just before sunset, deepest blue. Several of us from Denise's workshop at Stanford are going to make dinner together. Denise and I wait in my car while the others duck into a grocery store. A '66 Mustang convertible brought from Texas, the top is down. Looking up at the low hanging trees, a jay flying over, she bounces up and down and claps her hands. "How marvelous!

There's no roof! Look how much we can see!" She does this all the time. A regal sixty-six-year-old woman exclaiming and clapping her hands in delight.

> Every day, every day I hear enough to
> fill a year of nights with wondering.
>
> —from "Every Day"
> *Breathing the Water* (1984)

Nine of us in our Stegner Fellowship workshop at Stanford. Very different experiences, ages, poetics. Denise teaches us during the winter quarter each of the two years we are there. The Gulf War happens in our second year together. Denise organizes Stanford Poets for Peace, oversees the making of buttons and banners, leads the fellows and others of her students on San Francisco marches against the war. One of our younger colleagues says that for the first time she sees how to put her writing and her politics together.

> Politics,
> the word I use to mean
> striving for justice and for
> mercy.
>
> —from "The Phonecall"
> *Life in the Forest* (1975)

> ...I believe in the essential interrelatedness and mutual reinforcement of the meditative and the active.
>
> —from the Preface
> *The Poet in the World*

Yes, she could be uncompromising, especially when it came to natural detail. If a certain plant was referred to in a poem, she might raise a question as to whether that particular plant could indeed be found in that particular place at that particular time of year. Tomes must be consulted. It would not do to get it wrong, to take more liberties with nature than already exhibited in the human species' appalling lack of environmental consciousness.

And sometimes in discussion she would assert her views about a piece so strongly that it left no room for others'. The writer's feelings might be hurt. Denise, told about it later, would become anxious, bewildered, sad. She hadn't meant to hurt anyone, surely, only to say what she felt. She didn't know her own strength, the way her vitality commanded.

As a child she'd been schooled at home in London, adored by her parents and her poet sister Olga, nine years older. Her mother was a Welsh teacher and her father a Russian rabbinical student (of Sephardic roots) turned scholarly Anglican minister. The whole family was steeped in the arts and learning. Denise was precocious. How not? Had tea with her parents and Paul Robeson at eight. Hung around the stage door at Covent Garden at eleven or twelve, catching glimpses of Sir Thomas Beecham and the ballerinas she so wanted to grow up to be. At twelve, unbeknownst to her parents, volunteered to distribute *The Daily Worker*. Also at twelve, sent some of her poems to T.S. Eliot, who replied encouragingly.

> A child, no-one to stare, I'd run full tilt
>   to a tree,
> hug it, hold fast, loving the stolid way it
> stood there, girth
> arms couldn't round,
>   the way
> only the wind made it speak, gave it
> an autumn ocean of thoughts . . .

> if I came to a brook, off came my shoes,
> looking could not be enough—
> or my hands at least must be boats or
>   fish for a minute,
> to know the purling water at palm
>   and wrist.
>
>   —from "Metamorphic Journal"
>   *Life in the Forest* (1975)

That seamlessness again. She did not cross picket lines. She'd taught at several universities on the East Coast before moving to Seattle in 1989, at one of them long enough to be enrolled in a pension plan—"from which she withdrew in vocal disgust, on discovering a number of the university's investments conflicted with her principles. It was a costly scruple. At Stanford, she enrolled in a socially responsible plan. Protested every spring at the nuclear test site, though the desert taxed her physical energies tremendously.

> All of my dread and all of my longing
>   hope that Earth
> may outwit the huge stupidity of its
>   humans,
> can find their signs and protests here,
>   their recapitulations
> of joy and awe ...
>
>   —from "The Almost-Island"
>   *Evening Train* (1990)

One of the most profoundly sensuous beings I've ever known. Something animal, something organic, rooted in religious faith. There it is again: organic form. When she hugged you, it was not the quick abrazo learned during her years in Mexico. It was slow, encircling, a very still and silent holding, as though to hear and feel the life coursing through you. Almost always followed by a satisfied, "Mmmmmmm." She approved of the life coursing through you. Like the trees in childhood.

When she laughed, she rocked back and forth, often holding herself, as if to keep one wild energy of her peals and cackles from carrying her straight up into the air. And her laughter had a mischievous streak, as when she pointed it at a klutzy squirrel that had lost its balance and was swinging crazily upside down on a clothesline.

She did not merely look at things. She *went into* them. Seemed to take them apart molecule by molecule, inspecting the insides, the undersides, their previous forms. She would get very quiet looking at plants or light, at painting or sculpture, and I confess that the precious times we looked at nature or art together, I was as much entranced by her process of seeing as by what we saw. "Exciting the molecules" is perhaps more than a function of physics.

Because of her early love of dance, her years of training in ballet, she had a highly developed sense of gesture, those in poems and paintings, surely, and especially those of individuals. She hated talking on the telephone ("my telephone phobia") because so much of the real conversation was lost without the gestures of face and body.

She loved it when I said her name in Greek: *Dionysía*. Dthee-oh-nee-see-ah. That it implied respect for the earth. And our friend with whom she studied piano during her Stanford days, says much of her uninhibited child-joy poured out during those lessons. But there was also a profound reserve, a heavy curtain that often fell over certain private matters. Illness, for instance. Nothing to do with what others deemed "proper." More, it was about not wanting to "put people out"—and an almost animal sense of privacy.

That's how her death sneaked up on us, I think. A combination of that deep reserve and her heroic will to be alive, fully alive, absolutely as long as possible. She didn't enter the hospital until a week before she died, and I'm convinced she willed herself (and us) not to experience a slow, painful going. Gift-giving until the very last.

And beyond. We have twenty-three books of poems, inextricably linked: love poem, nature poems, political poems, poems of faith. Four books of essays, two of translation. And we have surely one of the best examples that ever been set for a life of unshakable integrity. Now it's up to us to make a better world, clap our hands, stand open-mouthed, be brought to speech.

Poet Rosemary Catacalos, whose roots are in San Antonio, is a former Stegner fellow, currently an affiliated scholar at Stanford's Institute for Research on Women and Gender. She thanks Carlene Carrasco Laughlin, Anne-Marie Cusac, Emily Warn, and Sara Doniach for helping her talk through this piece.

TRIBUTE TO ROSEMARY

Graciela Sanchez

From Rosemary's Memorial Service

> Salias del templo un día llorona,
> Cuando al pasar yo te vi
> Hermoso huipil llevavas llorona
> Que la virgin te creí

I first met Rosemary through remnants that she left behind at the rear apartment of 630 Mission St. I was moving in. Sandra Cisneros was moving out. And before Sandra, Rosemary had graced this little casita in Baja King William. I was escaping an abusive relationship, and here in this sweet casita were delicate and graceful pedacitos de white embroidered textiles that had been left behind by Rosemary. I finally got to meet her as the literature director of the Guadalupe Cultural Arts Center, where she helped push for the Hijas del Quinto Sol literary conference and other great literature programs, but Rosemary was on her way out to San Francisco, while I was returning home to San Antonio.

> Ay de mi Llorana, Llorona
> Llorana de ayer y hoy
> Ayer maravilla fui Llorona, y ahora ni sombra soy

Fortunately, for all of us, she came back home and then did what few working artists do. She took on the role of arts administrator as Executive Director of Gemini Ink. For me, this work showed her understanding of the need to nurture other writers, not just promote herself. One can always shine and be loved for genius within one's creative discipline, but to dedicate many years of her life to support and strengthen literary arts organizations, to find funding to hire other individual artists to work or to create workshops to strengthen and develop their skills or connect them to funding opportunities or other mentors, well . . . that took away from her own artistic creations. But she knew she couldn't be selfish and think only of her artistic production. It had to be about all of us growing, about strengthening and giving voice and space to the many young people who needed to be seen and heard. Not just one Latina Poet Laureate, but hundreds of us. Because we've only just begun truly writing and creating the more complex and brilliant stories that counter the hateful stereotypes that have buried us in shame and self-hatred. Rosemary knew this and so she gave it back as an arts administrator, which most see as a bureaucratic job; she knew and saw it as a very powerful role to build and make progressive and loving social change.

Rosemary was a social justice warrior connecting Black, brown, white, Asian, Arab and Native communities together. She was saving the Edwards Aquifer with her poetry, challenging the racism, sexism and patriarchy of our world. I remember that when Esperanza worked with Eastside residents and other community members to save the Hays Street Bridge from being privatized and lose 360 degree views of San Antonio from the Bridge, Rosemary graced us with poetry as we opened up a new venue for performances from the Hays Street Bridge. I remember chatting a few minutes after she got there and she asked for a chair. I found it and she sat down. She had recently been told that she had cancer and I didn't understand how she could be with us that day. But Rosemary understood that all of us needed to be part of this struggle as well. It was a seven-year struggle and while most disappeared from the work, Rosemary continued to be engaged and supported us, even at a distance when she could no longer be with us at the Bridge or the Courthouse.

With Rosemary's death, the world lost a fierce, beloved, committed, and loving mujer. With her legacy, we pledge to carry on the struggle for peace and justice here in San Antonio and throughout the world. Thank you for carrying on.

> No se que tienen las flores Llorona
> Las flores del campo santo
> Que cuando las mueve el viento Llorona
> Paracen que están llorando
>
> Ay de mi Llorona, Llorona
> Llorona de Azul celeste
> Y aunque me queste la vida llorona
> No dejaré de quererte

Rosemary Catacolos Presente! Rosemary Catacalos Ahora y Siempre!

Homesteaders
Rosemary Catacalos

for the Edwards Aquifer

They came for the water,
came to its sleeping place
here in the bed of an old sea,
the dream of the water.
They sank hand and tool into
soil where the bubble of springs
gave off hope, fresh and long,
the song of the water.
Babies and crops ripened
where they settled,
where they married their sweat
in the ancient wedding,
the blessing of the water.
They made houses of limestone
and adobe, locked together blocks
descended from shells and coral,
houses of the bones of the water,
shelter of the water.
And they swallowed the life
of the lime in the water,
sucked its mineral up
into their own bones
which grew strong as the water,
the gift of the water.

All along the counties they lay,
mouth to mouth with the water,
fattened in the smile of the water,

the light of the water,
water flushed pure through the
spine and ribs of the birth of life,
the old ocean,
the stone,
the home of the water.

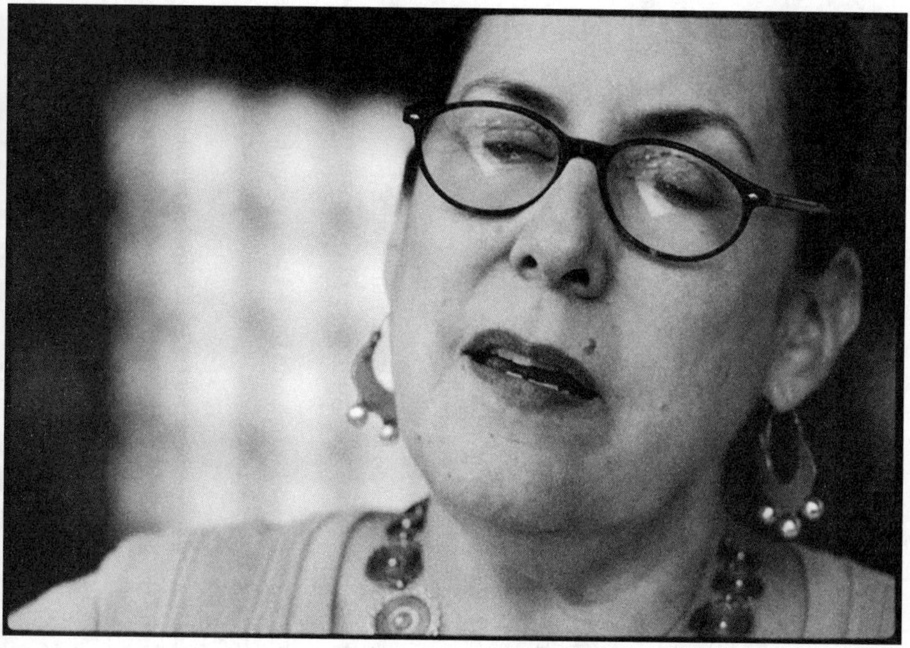

Women Talk of Flowers at Dusk
Rosemary Catacalos

San Antonio, Texas, 1976
Mérida, Yucatán, 1909

Some things can only be spoken in the dark, you'd say each time you told about Dolores,
a name that means pain. We'd sit in dimming light at the chipped kitchen table where the past

showed in layers of old paint: exile from *México*, your forced marriage, the Great Depression.
You with a cigarette and a shot of *Paul Jones*, a brittle voice, telling how your mother died

in the cheap half-light of rented rooms in the Turks' *barrio*. She was a nurse who
recognized the blood she coughed, but called it roses to ease your fears. Huacha was twelve and you, ten.

Even then you led. You hid in the jacaranda, fierce with tears, and barred your grandfather
when he arrived too late in his fancy carriage and fine frock coat. *Usted no tiene porqué*

estar aquí. No right to come here. You would always despise the jacaranda. *Mi madre muerta.*
¡Muerta! ¿Y él? He sent for pins to hold the sheet tight to the body. The first Indian doctor

in Merida, he'd raised his daughter to be a lady, not his fault she'd come to this. He wouldn't look at her wasted frame, the flowers lining her face, the borrowed crucifix. She'd refused to stay

well-married, would not respect his choice and turn a deaf ear, blind eye, the other cheek to a husband cajoling conquests behind palm fans, his seed spent in every street. Instead,

she'd made her own life in this damp *barrio*, nursing a company of women, the poor, everything the father struggled to forget. The funeral wagon stopped at the corner, too wide

for the narrow alley. You, your sister, some Indian women, wept at the gate. Only men were allowed at the grave, but he would not go. Yet he couldn't escape the wild marigold

that fell from her temple as they hoisted her onto the pauper's dray. That sight was a slap, Grandmother, that stung his face then and every time you told the story. Even now the flame

of that marigold is in me, you gone these many years, Dolores almost a century. So, too, it's come to me to heal the roses in the blood, to let go of the sins of the fathers,

open the dark vaults of the heart. Let me begin here, in lives that are and are not my own, to forgive even the jacaranda that blooms and blooms without mercy.

Memory in the Making: A Poetics
Rosemary Catacalos

for Lorna Dee Cervantes

Remember the tale where the maiden lets down her long, charged hair for the lover, his climb to her tower hanging by golden threads, by the very roots of her dreams?

This is not that story, which even then was vague about who, if anyone, was saved. No, we are just past what some call, without irony, the American Century.

At my university, students who own Beemers ride bikes into the fields for Earth Sciences while brown men from another country bike to other fields for food.

The students remember this, the brown men that. They are not the same. I say this as plain fact, though many hold sincerity has been cheapened in our complex age.

A little girl called Shelly weeps on her way to the school bus. She wears jellies, cheap plastic copies of a Greek fisherman's sandal. She spoke Spanish before English,

her Salvadoran nana, her parents at work. Pink keys, purple keychains, clank against her turquoise backpack. She did not dream last night. Tearstained, she

watches a family of lizards careen around the bleached trunk of a dead redwood, limbs bleached bones in the Wedgwood bowl of the sky. I can't see children

these days without asking what they'll remember of all this. Am I Shelly's
Miss Frances, strange neighbor woman who dressed me in shawls and sang

sadly in German? Whose husband, it was told, went up in flames on the Hindenburg?
How do we know what will touch a child, mark her forever? Remember the girls

in their pale summer dresses? Remember the women they became? And then there's
the memory locked in the cells, in the blood. Certainly potatoes are a kind of faith

to the Irish. Also recall Poland, someone's grandfather escaping under his mother's
skirts, this cliché all that's left of being Polish, Jewish, poor. Even so, the moment

still somewhere in the bone: potato stubble, smoke, strong smell of a woman's skirts,
becoming Catholic. Gazing at grandmother, what did she know, and how did she learn it?

And now we are everywhere and nowhere: videophones, internet. No borders
in the air, fresh blood on the ground. How to dance? Where does memory go

in all this? To work, emplumada! ¡A la chancla! We wear the black velvet hat
that came with the dream, loosen our tongues with the fire of roasted chiles.

The Greek women of Souli danced off the cliff of their village to keep out of the hands
of the Turks. And here we are on the purple lip of the cañon, telling and

there's no such thing as going too near the sun. Each time and each time the first. Just
past the close of the American Century, the child's plastic keys rattle down the street.

Perfect Attendance: Short Subjects Made from the Staring Photos of Strangers
Rosemary Catacalos

for Kiff Slemmons

The hand has its dreams, too, and its own hypotheses. It helps us to come to know matter in its secret inward parts.
—Gaston Bachelard

Suppose, in the old sense, they are waiting, expecting these loose silver frames
to dissolve in a million scenes, different every time and yet familiar, sponges

brought up from the dream floor, cuttings spliced into the blueing grain of closeup,
and careful backward steps toward the big picture, bringing what we can into view.

As when someone's Uncle Theo, his name the old Greek joke of "Uncle Uncle,"
misjudges his scythe-like sponge knife beneath the reef at Tarpon Springs

and bright red ribbons stream into this foreign sea from his bleeding hand,
the one that puts food on the table, and down in that pain he thinks of spring

and how his island blooms shore to shore, red poppies his grandfather told him
are every drop of blood ever shed in a war. If I've said this last before, forgive

what can't be said too many times. And, then, the hand that wears a crocheted glove sometimes removes the glove and smokes, sometimes smokes with the glove

on, both years later and in another life, for the crocheted glove is first supremely drawn to wild violets in a Texas pecan bottom on mornings still cool at seven,

violets set in a small pink glass at the bedside of the old woman who coughs and will not come back, even a lifetime later when the crocheted gloves are bought

in a thrift shop and taken out dancing where women smoke. Such as an older schoolmate named Olga whose right hand blurs at the register, this is the fifties

when the keys are round and rimmed with silver: dry beans, milk, thin tortillas, she rings me up so fast, chimes the sum, left hand flashing a tiny diamond and

her long reach down the counter for a bag stop-framed over and over in the air, a many-armed goddess who one day is not in school because her father has died

under a train in the roundhouse a few blocks away, his grease-streaked right hand still clutching a wrench. What if finally neither art nor life is imitation,

and each waits everywhere, full-blown, but needing the gift of perfect attendance: a twirling red skirt, work boots coated with clay mud, a weathered ladder left askew

near a pear tree in afternoon sun, basket nearby, whatever we cherish, we save. Muybridge's incessant horses, the clock covering its mysterious face with its hands.

"PRAISE THEM"

Poem by Li-Young Lee
Music by Rosemary Catacalos, Bett Butler, and Joël Dilley

Rosemary's poetry and reading exhibited a natural ear for music, and we often talked about words' inherent rhythm and pitch. When she asked bassist/composer Joël Dilley and me to create jazz settings for her reading of visiting writer Li-Young Lee's poetry for performances at the Ursuline Academy Chapel and Poetry at Round Top, she decided—with Lee's enthusiastic permission—to set a couple of his poems to music. We worked together in the studio, with her singing and me transcribing at the piano; and "Praise Them," with its lovely lyrics and lilting 6/8 swing, later found a place on my album *Myths & Fables*.

—Bett Butler

Bop Physics I. & II.
Rosemary Catacalos

I.
Solve for the unknown. Include every
        lost scrap of human history.
Begin here. That was yesterday.
Begin here again. That's today
        and every day.
Solve for the particle that is and is not
the same thing at the same time.
Might this explain human folly?
Solve for the fact that 95% of matter
        is unknown so cannot be described
or understood in any way.

Might this *ordain* human folly
        until we get good at knowing?
Will we get good in time?
        What will be its signature?
Solve for how the mockingbird perfectly recreates
the cardinal's call and the grackle's screech
        in the same breath, then perches atop the chimney
filling the house with a straight ahead bop
that brings Bird back to life.

II.
Solve for the blue shine of the butterfly's wing
that when touched by sunlight is capable
of lifting one-hundred times its weight in flight.
Factor in the inescapable fact that time stops
at the speed of light. Then go figure
what Prine meant with that bit about
the speed of loneliness. Keep going.
Always and without pause keep going.

So many thoughts, so little time.
Solve, resolve, revolve, recall how
every living thing is an infinity,
also every inanimate object.
Keep close to the bass.
Try not to miss a beat.

ON "BOP PHYSICS"

Mike Greenberg

> *After reading the poem "Bop Physics I. & II.," Mike Greenberg wrote the following note to Rosemary Catacalos:*

I must say, "Bop Physics I. & II." wrapped me in its tentacles as effectively as anything you've written, maybe more effectively than anything else you've written. It is a very brief Mahler symphony, being about absolutely everything while at the same time being about only one crucial thing. At the level of craft, even before I came to the Bird reference, I noted that the poem's rhythms and phrase lengths (short, staccato phrases leading into extended fluid runs) perfectly exemplified the title's "bop." The voice in this poem is pitched conspicuously higher than your usual, in keeping with Bird's alto sax. The weaving of allusive threads in parallel is especially wonderful.

By the way, you are surely aware of the very close resemblance of Charlie Parker's most frequently repeated rhythmic device to Woody Woodpecker's laugh. (That device appears prominently in Bird's earliest private recording—of "Honeysuckle Rose"—which was probably made within a year before or after the November 25, 1940, release of "Knock Knock," Woody Woodpecker's cinematic début.) But I suppose putting Woody into the poem might have somewhat shifted the coloration.

David Talamántez on the Last Day of Second Grade
Rosemary Catacalos

San Antonio, Texas 1988

David Talamántez, whose mother is at work, leaves his mark everywhere in the schoolyard,
tosses pages from a thick sheaf of lined paper high in the air one by one, watches them

catch on the teachers' car bumpers, drift into the chalky narrow shade of the water fountain,
one last batch, stapled together, he rolls tight into a makeshift horn through which he shouts

David! and *David, yes!* before hurling it away hard and darting across Brazos Street against
the light, the little sag of head and shoulders when, safe on the other side, he kicks a can

in the gutter and wanders toward home. David Talamántez believes birds are warm blooded,
the way they are quick in the air and give out long strings of complicated music, different

all the time, not like cats and dogs. For this he was marked down in Science, and for putting
his name in the wrong place, on the right with the date, *not* on the left with Science Questions,

and for not skipping a line between his heading and his answers. The X's for wrong things
are big, much bigger than David Talamántez's tiny writing. *Write larger,* his teacher has said

in red ink across the tops of many pages. *Messy!* she says on others where he has erased
and started over, erased and started over. Spelling, Language Expression, Sentences Using

the Following Words. *Neck. I have a neck name. No! 20's, 30's. Think again! He's good* in Art, though, makes 70 on Reading Station Artist's Corner, where he's traced and colored

an illustration from *Henny Penny*. A goose with red-and-white striped shirt, a hen in a turquoise dress. Points off for the birds, cloud and butterfly he's drawn in freehand. *Not in the original*

picture! Twenty-five points off for writing nothing in the blank after *This is my favorite scene in the book because*. . . . There's a page called Rules. *Listen! Always working! Stay in your seat!*

Raise your hand before you speak! No fighting! Be quiet! Rules copied from the board, no grade, only a giant red checkmark. Later there is a test on Rules. *Listen! Alay ercng! Sast in ao snet!*

Rars aone bfo your spek! No fmagn! Be cayt! He gets 70 on Rules, 10 on Spelling. An old man stoops to pick up a crumpled drawing of a large family crowded around a table, an apartment

with bars on the windows in Alazán Courts, a huge sun in one corner saying, *Too much noys!* The grade is 90. *Nice details!* And there's another mark, on this paper and all the others, the one

in the doorway of La Rosa Beauty Shop, the one that blew under the pool table at La Tenampa, the ones older kids have wadded up like big spit balls, the ones run over by cars. On every single

page David Talamántez has crossed out the teacher's red numbers and written in huge letters, blue ink, *Yes! David, yes!*

Texas In Transition

One of the panelists used the term "local vision." I think that local vision could be a danger for us.

Grim as it seems to me, economics is the only real projection for the future, unless it is true that something of the spirit can animate a people. We have heard here that we Texans are tired of the old mythology, the old frontier icons -- they don't represent us anymore and they don't animate us.

But it's difficult to build and recognize a new sustaining belief, if that is what a myth is in the positive sense -- you don't do it by getting up an ad campaign.

More than two roads now are diverging in the woods of our world. Whatever roads Texas takes, they must put it in the larger world. That will be the true transition, and matters of the spirit -- of humility, empathy, understanding, hope for others as well as ourselves, a sense of shared humanity -- must be part of that linking of Texas to the world.

I think that one of the truly important things that happened in Texas this year was that Rosemary Catacalos, a San Antonio poet, had children in the grade schools write message-poems of sympathy and encouragement to the children of the earthquake in Mexico City. Whatever the economic future, that kind of act and understanding must be a major asset of a new Texas, because it helps us to understand, also, our new diversity and the reality of our situation.

-- Marshall Terry

Shelving Rose Catacalos
Jim LaVilla-Havelin

so, yes, really this shelving thing is about some odd
        juxtapositions, and some fitting
and about fitting together the odd ones
to make some kind of sense—a balancing act
        between or a shared energy
                of words

you fit neatly on the film shelves between
        Buñuel and Cocteau
on the art shelves between
        Mary Cassatt and Judy Chicago
           though I'm hard-pressed to find Cézanne
and among the CDs between Eva Cassidy and
              John Coltrane

hardest to figure, the vast plain of the collections
        shelf between Charles Bukowski and
        Robert Coles, that'll teach 'em a
            thing or two

snug on the Latinx shelves between
        Ana Castillo and Denise Chavez,
           there's sisterhood
           for you

the regular shelves make space for you
        between Joyce Cary and Willa Cather
        a place of story unfolding,
           words of wonder

and on the poetry shelves, where there is really
>no one like you, no one with the heart and
muscle and ear,
>>you rest between
>>Raymond Carver and Catullus

be there and there and there, dear one, so much
>more
>>than everything.

Red Dirt, Atascosa County, Texas
Rosemary Catacalos

en memoria, Rafael Peñaloza Macedo

If in a field of wild sweet smells, if digging peanuts in red dirt, if the *comadre*
in the shack at the bend in the road brings her six children out to whistle and wave,

if the old horse is not ours, if the red boots take the *tía* dancing but not to the altar,
if the trails the cows make in mesquite brush, if the mystery of the farm just across

where the man does not speak and sits in the sun with his eyes shut and arms
he can't lift hanging at his sides, still as his children's rusty swings. If the terror

of the bull's red eyes the night it charges the flimsy wood cart where we sleep,
if one day Carlos falls from the horse that is not ours and has to see an Anglo doctor

in Devine who doesn't much care, if the children dream hideouts and labyrinths
on the trails the cows make in mesquite brush, if no one can find the lone child

who believes there is nothing so safe as sunlight, how it touches everything, but not the wrong way. If digging peanuts, if growing sunflowers for chicken feed,

if digging and digging the well, if the grandfather believed this would save them, if the city, if its broken glass, if the struggle makes good people do bad things, if you

can breathe when you say this. If the Hereford's white faces hide in tule fog by their water hole until someone staring hard can make them out, if a man who

can't move his arms smiles when his closed eyelids blaze red inside each time the sun comes out from behind a cloud, if he noticed this when he was a child,

if it helps at all. If, digging peanuts, a sharp clod of red dirt bruises your haunches when you fall back off your ankles into the high blue sky, if you laugh. If years

later you buy red boots and set out to find the grandfather's favorite tree, ancient broad liveoak standing alone in the middle of the widest field in all sixteen

acres meant to save us. If, passing the empty shack at the bend in the road, you wave, you by God whistle.

RED FOR ROSEMARY

Jim LaVilla-Havelin

Across a long drought and years without her, the dirt of Atascosa County emerges as grasses burn off. If winds would come, the century plant stalks should fall, and red dirt would fly into our faces. But these are my ifs, not Rosemary's. And Rosemary's ifs across the long lines of her "Red Dirt, Atascosa County, Texas" are not the tentative squirrelly ifs of Cummings. These ifs are really whens.

In the penultimate couplet of this ground-breaking (pun-intended) poem, across the passage of time, she buys red boots. The funnel of time and circumstance collapses in on me. The first time I saw Rosemary Catacalos she had come home to San Antonio in the late '90s to read as part of the Guadalupe's Inter-American Book Fair, held that year in the Henry B. Gonzalez Convention Center.

Rosemary on stage was commanding, beautiful, funny, unlike anyone I'd ever heard (and that is still my assertion), and dressed festively, all the way down to her red boots. And while, unlike the Moira Shearer red shoes, they did not keep her dancing on forever, they flashed her persistent brilliance, her impressive grin. And she passed them on to the next Latino Texas State Poet Laureate, Carmen Tafolla. They now reside at the Wittliff Collection.

It is one amazement of "Red Dirt, Atascosa County, Texas" that blood, which runs through it, kinship, connection, is never mentioned. Hear it, though, in the couplet which reads, in part,

> if the grandfather believed the world would save them, if
> the city, if its broken glass, if the struggle makes good people do bad things . . .

And it is in blood, blood ties, the pulsing sympathy of a Greek-Latina, both understanding something of the lives of others and trying to puzzle out their connection, their difference that she writes in the first poem of Begin Here (of which "Red Dirt, Atascosa County, Texas" is the penultimate poem) "Women Talk of Flowers at Dusk":

> Let me begin here, in lives that are and are not my own,
>   to forgive even the jacaranda that blooms and blooms
>   without mercy.

Rosemary's is a fierce poetry. A poetry of outrage, justice, voices of the unheard, and unwillingness to bend to simple fashion. It is a poetry that ranges from "Katakalos" and its
domestic, family history account—

> Still they must have had a
> little something special going.
> Seeing as how back then
> he spoke only Greek,
> a little broken English,
> and she spoke only Spanish.

> They were married through an interpreter

—to the boldly risky colloquial-voiced homage to Maya Angelou in "Swallow Wings," with its glorious and graceful finish:

> Swallows keep making' their wings
> out to be commas on the sky.
> World keeps sayin' and, and, and, and,
> and.

This is a poetry that alerts us to the balance of lines both long and short. She measured them out, amazingly enough, against what she had to say—a careful balance of both sound and sight. It is a poetry that ranges even to the much beloved anthem for the misbegotten student at the hands of an unsympathetic teacher in "David Talamantez on the Last Day of Second Grade." (Catacalos taught poetry to young people, along with Naomi Nye and many others of us.). Poetry lives in David's voice, his resistance, his resilience, his empowerment.

It is, across lines that break and overlap and take the fullness of the page, as Rosemary hears and crystallizes music, that the sharp edge, the refining lens is so clear. In "Bop Physics I & II" she writes,

> Solve, resolve, revolve, recall how
> every living thing is an infinity...

and the word play, the consciousness of the depth and resonance of neighborly words, opens up that very infinity. So, too, in "Headscarf"—a compacted, knotted, later work.

I had a phone call from Rosemary days before she left us. Her great rich voice had thinned. She asked if I would be her literary executor and commit to assembling a volume of her unpublished poems to be entitled Sing! This volume is the beginning of that journey—and how to capture her, how within the lines, the voice, the powerful presence of Rose, to illuminate her—this fierce poet whose poems live, incandescent.

In her heartbreaking "In the Lands Where the Oldest Angels Have Always Known it Would Come to This, Aylan Tells of his Fleeting Two Years," Aylan, a small corpse on the beach (oh, she would be horrified at the scale of destruction, deaths of children, now, but understood the gravity of the single and specific image, the child) she writes, "a tiny bright red fish darting in sunlight." Rose—from red dirt to this flickering life-affirming-in-the-face-of-death fish, colors my time of her, a time extending outward even now—

These mornings, with Rose, alive in her words, I watch the cardinals at the feeder. And further down the driveway, though we were afraid the drought had killed it off, a little rain and there are leaves on our olive tree. She'd like that.

ROSEMARY CATACALOS: A CHRONOLOGY

March 18, 1944	born in St. Petersburg, Florida
1960s	reporter and arts columnist for the *San Antonio Light*
1984	publication of *As Long as it Takes* (Iguana Press)
	publication of *Again for the First Time* (Tooth of Time Books) (Received Texas Institute of Letters poetry prize)
1986-1989	director of the Literature Program at the Guadalupe Cultural Arts Center—expanded the Annual Texas Small Press Book Fair Into the San Antonio Inter-American Book Fair
1989-2003	California, Stegner Center Creative Writing Fellow at Stanford University
1991-1996	Executive Director, The Poetry Center / American Poetry Archives San Francisco State University Visiting Scholar at the Institute for Research on Women & Gender, Stanford University
1996	"David Talamàntez on the Last Day of Second Grade" selected by Adrienne Rich for *Best American Poetry*
2003	returns to San Antonio
2003-2012	Executive Director, Gemini Ink, Literary Arts Center, San Antonio
2003	"Perfect Attendance: Short Subjects Made from the Staring Photos of Strangers" selected by Yusef Komunyakaa for *Best American Poetry*
2008	receives the Macondo Foundation Elvira Cordero Cisneros Award

2013	first Latina Poet Laureate for the State of Texas
	Anniversary edition, *Again for the First Time* (Wings Press)
	Begin Here (Wings Press)
June 17, 2022	dies in San Antonio
Sept. 9, 2022	Memorial Service at the Carver Community Cultural Center

* A good biographical sketch from which much of this chronology is taken appears in *Literary San Antonio*, edited by Bryce Milligan (Texas Christian University Press, 2018).

CONTRIBUTORS

MAHA AHMED is a writer, editor, and translator. She is a Creative Writing PhD candidate at the University of Houston and a recipient of the 2021 Inprint Nina and Michael Zilkha Fellowship as well as winner of the 2023 Inprint Donald Barthelme Prize in Poetry. Her work has appeared in *Grist*, *The Adroit Journal*, *The Recluse*, and elsewhere.

MICHAEL ANANIA is a poet, fiction writer, essayist, and editor. His recent books are *Continuous Showings* (2017), *Nightsongs and Clamors* (2018), and *In Time* (2024). Anania lives in Austin, TX.

Poetry, music, video, and voiceover by BETT BUTLER AND JOËL DILLEY have appeared in print and online journals in the U.S., U.K., E.U., and Canada. Award-winning musicians, they co-own Mandala Music Production, where they produce original music licensed by HBO, Discovery Channel, and more. Their website is www.mandalamusic.com.

CARY CLACK is a *San Antonio Express-News* columnist and editorial writer. He was inducted into the Texas Institute of Letters in 2017. Two collections of his columns, *Clowns and Rats Scare Me* (2009) and *Finish Lines to Cross: Notes on Race, Redemption and Hope* (2024) have been published by Trinity University Press.

ANEL I. FLORES (they/her) is an artist, writer and queer activist Ama en South Texas. They are author of *Curtains of Rain*, *Empanada: A Lesbiana Story en Probaditas*, *Les Maestres*, chapbooks *La Fea* and *Behind the Bookbag*, and co-editor of *Jota* and *I Love Us*. Their first love was their grandma Olivia.

REGINALD GIBBONS is the author of the novel *Sweetbitter*, which won the Anisfield-Wolf Book Award, as well as the poetry collection *Creatures of a Day*, which was a Finalist for the National Book Award. Recipient of various other prizes and fellowships, his thirteenth book of poems is forthcoming from LSU Press in March 2025. He was the editor of *TriQuarterly Magazine* from 1981 to

1997, and taught at Northwestern University, having served as the Frances Hooper Professor of Arts and Humanities (now emeritus).

MIKE GREENBERG is a writer and photographer living in San Antonio. He was a critic and columnist for the *San Antonio Express-News* from 1979 to 2007. His friendship with Rosemary Catacalos spanned nearly four decades.

JIM LAVILLA-HAVELIN is the author of eight books of poetry, most recently, *Mesquites Teach us to Bend* (Lamar University Literary Press, 2025) and *The Thoreau Book* (Alabrava Press, 2025). Coordinator of National Poetry Month activities in San Antonio for over twenty years, LaVilla-Havelin is the Literary Executor for the estate of Rosemary Catacalos, currently editing ¡SING!, her unpublished poems.

Palestinian-American writer, editor and educator NAOMI SHIHAB NYE grew up in St. Louis, Jerusalem, and San Antonio. She has been Young People's Poet Laureate for the U.S. (Poetry Foundation), and a visiting writer in hundreds of schools and communities all over the world. Writer or editor of more than 30 books, in 2024 she received the Wallace Stevens Award from the Academy of American Poets and the Texas Writer Award.

DR. AARON ELLINGTON PRADO began studying classical piano at age 7 and added formal jazz study in high school, attending the Stanford Jazz Workshop. In 2014 Prado received a Doctor of Musical Arts from the University of Texas Austin's Butler School of Music. Longtime musical director of KRTU FM, he initiated the Jazz Poetry Week presentations, cohosted with Jim LaVilla-Havelin.

GEORGE PRADO has been a bassist, band leader, and educator for more than 40 years in San Antonio. George's own jazz ensemble, The Regency Jazz Band, founded in 1982, has performed in Jazz Alive, and at venues throughout San Antonio. He is an annual presence during Jazz Poetry Week on KRTU FM with Jim LaVilla-Havelin.

GRACIELA ISABEL SÁNCHEZ follows in the footsteps of her mother and abuelitas, strong neighborhood women of color cultural workers and activists of San Antonio, TX. As a Buena gente of the Esperanza Peace and Justice Center, a community-based cultural arts/social justice organization, Graciela works with staff and community to develop programs that culturally ground working class and poor people of color, queer people and women, individuals who are survivors of cultural genocide.

ANIS SHIVANI'S books of fiction, poetry, and criticism include, most recently, *Literary Writing in the 21st Century: Conversations, Confessions: Poems, Logography: A Poetry Omnibus,* and *A History of the Cat in Nine Chapters or Less: A Novel.*

IRE'NE LARA SILVA, 2023 Texas State Poet Laureate, is the author of five poetry collections: *furia, Blood Sugar Canto, CUICACALLI/ House of Song, FirstPoems,* and *the eaters of flowers.* She is also the author of a comic book, *VENDAVAL,* and a short story collection, *flesh to bone,* which won the Premio Aztlán. http://www.irenelarasilva.wordpress.com

ARTHUR SZE'S latest book of poetry is *Into the Hush* (Copper Canyon Press, 2025), and he is also the author of *The White Orchard: Selected Interviews, Essays, and Poems* (Museum of New Mexico Press, 2025). In 2024, he received the Rebekah Johnson Bobbitt National Prize for Poetry from the Library of Congress.

MARSHALL TERRY was a professor and administrator at Southern Methodist University, a novelist, and the founder of SMU's creative writing program. His novel, *Tom Northway,* was the co-winner of the Texas Institute of Letters top prize for the best novel of 1968.

DR. CARMEN TAFOLLA, author of 40 books, was named the State Poet Laureate of Texas in 2015. From 2012 – 2014 she served as the first City Poet Laureate of San Antonio, and in 2018 became the first Latina to be elected President of the Texas Institute of Letters. Winner of numerous literary awards, Tafolla is a poet, storyteller, performance artist, cultural activist, Professor Emeritus, and a native of San Antonio's West Side barrio.

ACKNOWLEDGEMENTS

Many of the poems in this volume were drawn from the three books Rosemary Catacalos published in her lifetime:

As Long as it Takes / Iguana Press / 1984
Again for the First Time / Wings Press / 1984, 2013
Begin Here / Wings Press / 2013

Other poems in this volume did not appear in any of her books, though they may have appeared in magazines, periodicals, and anthologies.

Rosemary's work also appeared in most of the Latina, Latinx, Texas and feminist anthologies of the 70s through the 90s. To compile a complete bibliography of where Rosemary's work appeared is a task for another day, but just a few of those anthologies are:

Daughters of the Fifth Sun: A Collection of Latina Fiction & Poetry edited by Bryce Milligan, Mary Guerrero Milligan & Angela de Hoyos / Riverhead Books / 1995

From Totmes to Hip Hop: A Multicultural Anthology of Poetry Across the Americas 1900 – 2002 edited by Ishmael Reed / Thunder's Mouth Press / 2003

Women Brave in the Face of Danger: Photographs and Writing by Latin and North American Women edited by Margaret Randall / Crossing Press / 1985

Best American Poetry 1996 / edited by Adrienne Rich / Scrivener
Best American Poetry 2003 / edited by Yusef Komunyakaa / Scrivener

We would like to thank Wings Press, *The San Antonio Express-News*, *The Texas Observer*, and the Wittliff Collection.

Further acknowledgements for photography, ephemera, and previously published work are as follows:

p. 25   Michael Anania's poem, "This Broken Song" was originally published in *In Time*, Madhat Press, 2024

pp. 31, 32, 55   Photographs by Carlos Rene Perez

p.54   This photograph by Carlos Rene Perez, titled "Cimitiere du Père Lachais," was the cover image for Rosemary Catacalos's first book, *As Long as it Takes*.

p. 73   The first section of Arthur Sze's essay, "Afterword to the Thirtieth Anniversay Edition" was initially published in the thirtieth anniversary edition of *Again for the First Time*. The second section of the essay was written for this volume.

p. 78   Anis Shivani's essay "Poems New and Old from Texas Poet Laureate Rosemary Catacalos" was originally Published in *The Texas Observer*, January 22, 2014.

p. 101   Rosemary Catacalos Papers, Accession 2024-014, Box #4351 File #11, The Wittliff Collections/Texas State University.

p. 108   Rosemary Catacalos Papers, Accession 2024-014, Box #4350 File #39, The Wittliff Collections/Texas State University.

p.111   Cary Clack's obituary of Rosemary, "Poet's Voice Will Live On in the World She Loved" was originally published in *San Antonio Express News*, June 24, 2022.

p.119   This image was the cover of the memorial service celebrating the life of Rosemary Catacalos.

p. 120   QR code links to "Mnemosyno (remastered):: A Tribute to Poet Rosemary Catacalos :: Music by Joël Dilley" https://www.youtube.com/watch?v=-arccTMrUQk&list=PPSV

p.123   Rosemary's obituary for Denise Levertov, "A Seamlessly Committed Life: Denise Levertov, 1923 – 1997" was originally published in *The Texas Observer*, February 13, 1998.

p.123 Rosemary Catacalos Papers, Accession 2024-014, Box #4354 File #9, The Wittliff Collections/Texas State University.

p. 135 Rosemary Catacalos Papers, Accession 2024-014, Box #4349 File #8, The Wittliff Collections/Texas State University.

p. 142 QR code links to "Praise Them" by Bett Butler from *Myths and Fables*. https://bettbutler.bandcamp.com/track/praise-them-2

p.147 QR code links to "Bop Physics" by Rosemary Catacalos read by Jim LaVilla-Havelin to music performed by Dr. Aaron Ellington Prado and George Prado. https://www.youtube.com/watch?v=YDjgDjeJ7LU

p. 148 Rosemary Catacalos Papers, Accession 2024-014, Box #4351 File #36, The Wittliff Collections/Texas State University.

p.151. "Poet Rosemary Catacalos at the 2016 Texas Book Festival in Austin, Texas" © 2016 Larry D. Moore.

THE UNSUNG MASTERS SERIES BOARD OF DIRECTORS

Wayne Miller, Director
UNIVERSITY OF COLORADO AT DENVER

Kevin Prufer, Director
UNIVERSITY OF HOUSTON

Martin Rock, Director
UNIVERSITY OF CALIFORNIA AT SAN DIEGO

Kazim Ali
UNIVERSITY OF CALIFORNIA AT SAN DIEGO

Sarah Ehlers
UNIVERSITY OF HOUSTON

Niki Herd
WASHINGTON UNIVERSITY

Benjamin Johnson
UNIVERSITY OF CENTRAL MISSOURI

Joanna Luloff
UNIVERSITY OF COLORADO AT DENVER

Jenny Molberg
UNIVERSITY OF CENTRAL MISSOURI

Adrienne Perry
VILLANOVA UNIVERSITY

THIS EDITION OF THE UNSUNG MASTERS
IS PRODUCED AS A COLLABORATION AMONG:

Gulf Coast: A Journal of Literature and Fine Arts
and
Copper Nickel
and
Pleiades: Literature in Context

GENEROUS SUPPORT AND FUNDING PROVIDED BY:

University of Houston Department of English
Debbie Gary
Inprint Houston

This book is set in Adobe Aldine with Avenir
essay titles and Lato page numbers.

In the Lands Where the Oldest Angels Have Always Known It Would Come to This, Aylan Tells of His Fleeting Two Years

Rosemary Catacalos

What work to learn pomegranate and olive, tell
blue from green! The little brown dog lived down
the way, then was gone. All moved loud and quickly.
Some nights Mama's hand trembled as she did
her long braid. *All praise,* and *inshalláh* said the old
neighbor woman. *I will stay in this packed earth
house where I was born, my mother, grandfather.
May you go in peace!* Baba had scolded that sitting
tired by the roadside would not get us there. And
there was everything! *There* you wore special
clothes and behaved your best. On the way
there you took fine naps on the sand, could
trade unbroken shells with Galip. And then in
that odd silence of Baba's hand slipping away,
there was a shining half-split-second of delight:
holy blue, wild fig green, and so help me by Alláh,
a tiny bright red fish darting in sunlight. Such sunlight!

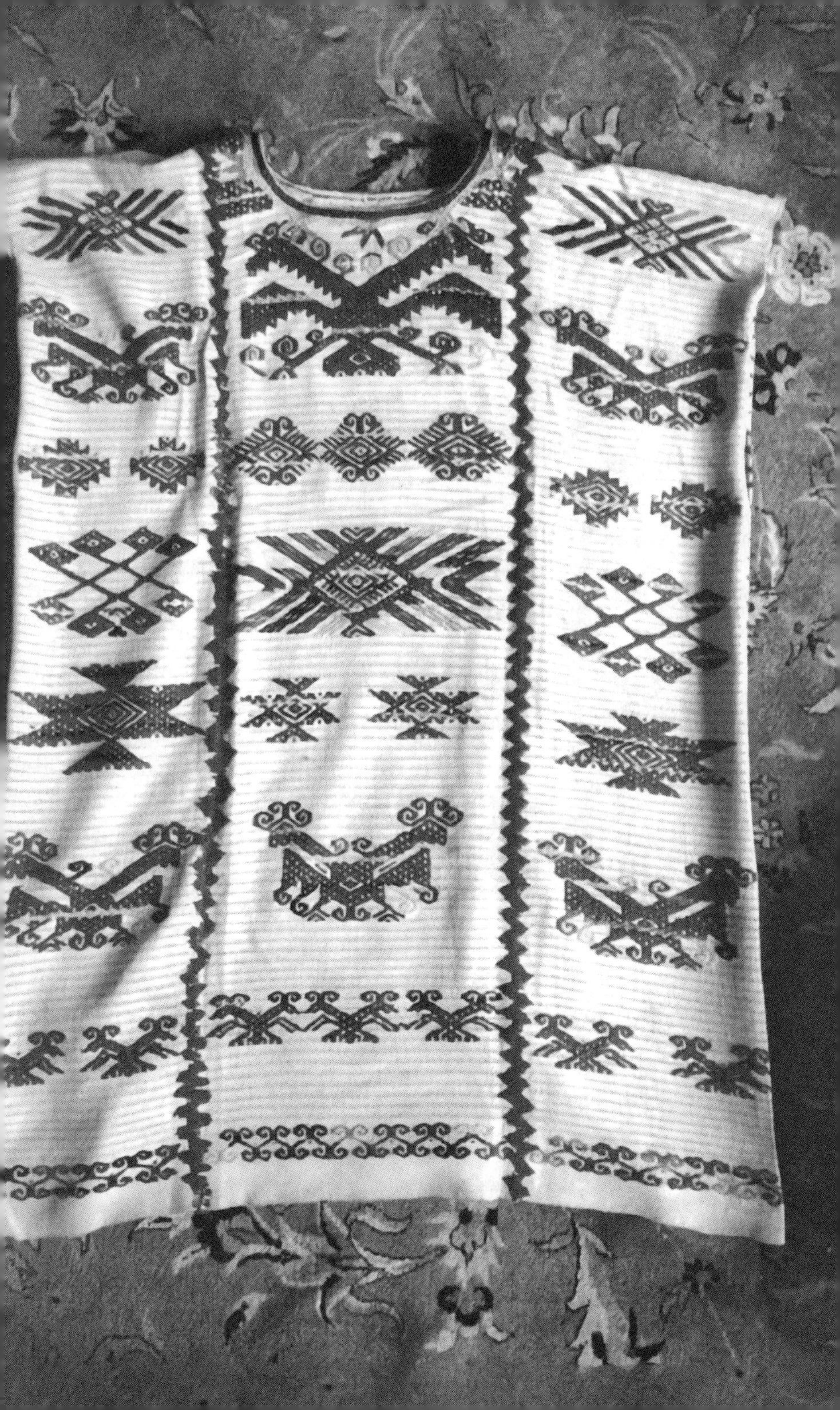